Selected titles from Women in Religion

Christian Women in Indonesia: A Narrative Study of Gender and Religion
Frances Adeney

Emma Curtis Hopkins: Forgotten Founder of New Thought
Gail M. Harley

Emma Newman: A Frontier Woman Minister
Randi Jones Walker

Moon Sisters, Krishna Mothers, Rajneesh Lovers: Women's Roles in New Religions
Susan J. Palmer

Moravian Women's Memoirs: Related Lives, 1750–1820
Katherine M. Faull, trans. & ed.

Rational Mothers and Infidel Gentlemen: Gender and American Atheism, 1865–1915
Evelyn Kirkley

Why Me, Lord? One Woman's Ordination to the Priesthood With Commentary and Complaint
Reverend Betty Bone Schiess

Windows of Faith: Muslim Women Scholar-Activists of North America
Gisela Webb, ed.

Women in Korean Zen: Lives and Practices
Martine Batchelor and Son'Gyong Sunim

"Providence Has Freed Our Hands"

Women's Missions and the American Encounter with Japan

Karen K. Seat

Syracuse University Press

First Edition 2008
08 09 10 11 12 13 6 5 4 3 2 1

Publication of this book was made possible in part by the University of Arizona's Provost's Author Support Fund.

The paper used in this publication meets the minimum requirements of American National Standard for Information Sciences—Permanence of Paper for Printed Library Materials, ANSI Z39.48-1984.∞™

For a listing of books published and distributed by Syracuse University Press, visit our Web site at SyracuseUniversityPress.syr.edu.

ISBN-13: 978-0-8156-3181-1 ISBN-10: 0-8156-3181-2

Library of Congress Cataloging-in-Publication Data

Seat, Karen K.
"Providence has freed our hands" : women's missions and the American encounter with Japan. — 1st ed.
p. cm. — (Women in religion)
Includes bibliographical references and index.
ISBN 978-0-8156-3181-1 (hardcover : alk. paper) 1. Women in missionary work. 2. United States—Church history—19th century. 3. Russell, Elizabeth, 1836–1928. 4. Methodist Episcopal Church—Missions—Japan. 5. Missions—Japan. 6. Women missionaries—United States. I. Title.
BV2610.S43 2008
266'.7652082—dc22
2007040387

Manufactured in the United States of America

For my parents, Leroy and June Seat,
and for my husband, Robert Daoust

Karen K. Seat is an associate professor in the Religious Studies Program at the University of Arizona. She was born and raised in Fukuoka, Japan.

Contents

Illustrations

Acknowledgments

I am deeply appreciative of the numerous people who contributed to the process of creating this book. I would like to thank the faculty and staff at Kwassui Gakuin for their generosity in opening Kwassui's resources to me during my months of research in Japan. Kwassui teacher Patricia McCreary (now retired) has been especially helpful as she has shared her knowledge and passion regarding the history of Kwassui and the life of Elizabeth Russell.

I am indebted to the mentors I had early in my research, including Katie Geneva Cannon, Lucy Bregman, John Raines, and Kathleen Uno. My appreciation also goes out to my colleagues at the University of Arizona for their support and encouragement over the years, including Adele Barker, Robert Burns, Kathryn Chavez, Susan Crane, Peter Foley, Kathrin Maurer, Roxanne Mountford, Mary Voyatzis, Cynthia White, and others. Many thanks to Shannon L. C. Cate and C. L. Cole for their contributions to this process. I also would like to extend my gratitude to Amanda Porterfield, Glenn Wright, Linda Cuckovich, Marian Buda, and others involved with Syracuse University Press, who have made the publication of this book a reality.

Finally, my family certainly deserves recognition for their involvement in this project. My sister-in-law, Mina Seat, was invaluable in working with me as I conducted research in Japan and in providing assistance with the Japanese language. My parents, Leroy and June Seat, and my brother, Keith Seat, read drafts of this book at various stages. I also appreciated the encouragement I received from other family members, including Ken Seat, Kathy and Tim Laffoon, Brenda Seat, and Cécile and Jean Daoust.

My husband, Robert Daoust, not only provided useful feedback on the manuscript as it evolved, but was also a constant source of inspiration during the time it took to complete this book.

Funding for research leading to this publication was provided in part by the Research Enablement Program, a grant program for scholarship supported by The Pew Charitable Trusts, Philadelphia, Pennsylvania, and administered by the Overseas Ministries Study Center, New Haven, Connecticut. Additional funding for various stages of research and writing was provided by Temple University and the University of Arizona.

Introduction

At the turn of the nineteenth century, American Protestant women's foreign missionary work challenged Americans themselves to reexamine their ideological assumptions about gender, race, Christianity, and civilization. This book investigates the ways in which American Protestantism was reshaped by the rise of women's independent mission societies. These societies' widely circulated mission magazines exposed American households to the experiences of American women in cultures around the world, and thereby broadened ordinary Protestants' world views.

As this book reveals, U.S. religious and cultural history cannot be fully understood without placing it in the global context, illuminating sites of American cultural production both within and beyond U.S. national borders. The study of American missions proves most fruitful in understanding American global encounters as the United States developed into a world power. As numerous postcolonial theorists have argued,[1] the ramifications of global imperialism renders inadequate the concept of discrete "Western" and "non-Western" histories. Thus, this book, although much of it is set outside U.S. national boundaries, is largely about the evolution of American identities and institutions through cross-cultural interactions.

1. Frederick Cooper and Ann Laura Stoler, for example, state that the "focus on the historical importance of nation-states should not diminish the longer history of empires and the patterns by which elites and subalterns moved about within them. . . . [for example,] empire could complicate gender compromises at home" (1997, 23). Edward Said also argues that the history of the "Orient" is integral and internal to the history of the West (1993).

In this period, the American women who most often traveled overseas, and who had the most impact on Protestant thinking about gender and globalization, were the women who participated in foreign missions. As illustrated throughout this book, these women continuously crossed boundaries: They brought things meant to be kept in an imagined "private," domestic sphere out into the world—namely, their female bodies and "feminized" religion—and they brought the cultures of the world into the sacred haven of Protestant American homes through their popular mission magazines.

The popularity and influence of American women's missions during the United States' ascent as a world power reveals that Protestantism, gender ideologies, and expansionist fervor were intimately connected in U.S. history, albeit in frequently conflicted ways. The drive to spread Christianity and domestic ideals overseas ultimately changed the very shape of American Protestantism and domestic ideals back in the United States. Ironically, the widespread movement to globalize nineteenth-century middle-class Protestant ideals became part of the process by which these ideals changed and evolved.

Nowhere were middle-class Protestant ideals challenged more than in Japan—one of the most unnerving fields for mission work in this era, as Japan metamorphosed into an imperialist power in its own right. A significant portion of this book examines American women's missions in Japan, which, more than any other country during this era, forced American Protestants to rethink their assumptions about racial hierarchies and the superiority of "Christian" civilizations.

These themes can be seen in the life and work of Elizabeth Russell (1836–1928), a particularly colorful Methodist Episcopal missionary to Japan, whose story appears throughout this book as a window into the larger story. Russell's life microcosmically reflected key elements fueling American women's missions: the rise of women's higher education in the United States; the impact of evangelical spirituality on nineteenth-century women's identities and activities; the broadening horizons available to American women through U.S. expansionism; and the ever-growing challenge women posed to conservative American gender ideologies as a result of all this.

Elizabeth Russell's eightieth birthday picture, 1916. Courtesy of Kwassui Women's College.

Russell was employed as a professional missionary by the Woman's Foreign Missionary Society of the Methodist Episcopal Church (WFMS), one of the most powerful women's institutions of the late nineteenth century. As the WFMS became the largest independent women's foreign missionary society in the United States, it signaled a new era of American women's religious activity. Methodist Episcopal women missionaries were able to influence a large audience back in the United States. The monthly magazine published by the WFMS, titled *The Heathen Woman's Friend* (renamed *Woman's Missionary Friend* in 1896), reached tens of thousands of homes across the country, where American women who rarely traveled far from home could read about the adventures of those who did.

Russell was one of the most influential American missionaries in Japan during the late nineteenth century, as she founded an exceptionally progressive school for girls and women there, defying both the conservative gender ideologies of her own mission organization and the Japanese government. Russell's educational institution, Kwassui Jo Gakkō, became very popular with Japanese women seeking a higher education despite criticism from Japanese and Westerners alike. By the end of the century, as missionaries struggled to compete with Japanese-controlled schools, Russell's school became a model for other mission schools, and more conservative missionaries were compelled to move beyond their own gender ideologies in order to maintain a competitive edge in Japan.

Transformed by their overseas experiences, by the early twentieth century many missionaries involved in Japan and other countries began to speak more boldly in favor of expanding women's access to education, paid labor, and politics, and missionaries openly opposed overt racism in the United States. For example, missionaries vigorously worked against the growing anti-Japanese sentiments in the United States that ultimately led to the legal exclusion of Japanese in the Immigration Act of 1924. Americans who sought to maintain traditional hierarchies—such as those who promoted Japanese exclusion and opposed women's rights—at times even went so far as to identify missionaries as a danger to what they believed to be traditional American values.

As historians Grant Wacker and Daniel H. Bays point out,

> the foreign missionary enterprise illumines U.S. religious history with particular clarity. . . . It prompted the first sustained examination of age-old assumptions about Christian exclusivism, heightened the evangelism versus social gospel tension, aggravated the fundamentalist-modernist controversy, energized church fundraising techniques, sharpened entrepreneurial skills, sustained scores of Bible institutes and seminaries, and helped amplify and reconfigure women's opportunities. (2003, 1, 4)

This book seeks to further explore the American mission experience and its impact on American culture, revealing how missions triggered new discourses in the United States regarding gender and race.

In Japan, names are written with the family name first and the given name second; Japanese names appear this way in this book. When citing Japanese (or Chinese) authors writing in English, each author's preference is followed. Japanese place names familiar in English (such as Tokyo) appear without macrons.

Abbreviations

CCUSFM	Central Committee on the United Study of Foreign Missions
HWF	*The Heathen Woman's Friend*
MEC	Methodist Episcopal Church
MSMEC	Missionary Society of the Methodist Episcopal Church
TFJ	*Tidings from Japan*
WBM	Women's Board of Missions
WCTU	Woman's Christian Temperance Union
WFMS	Woman's Foreign Missionary Society of the Methodist Episcopal Church
WFMSPC	Woman's Foreign Missionary Society of the Presbyterian Church
WMF	*Woman's Missionary Friend*
WWW	*Woman's Work for Woman*

"Providence Has Freed Our Hands"

I

"Something in Me, Dangerous"

Women's Missions in the Age of Empire

"What shall we do with woman?" That is the question the ages have been asking. . . . Who ever asked "What shall we do with man?" It is assumed that his functions and sphere have been predetermined. That he can be safely trusted, in a general way, to follow his instincts. But woman is dependent; her instincts are capricious. It is unsafe to trust her. A social revolution or frightful cataclysm of some sort might ensue without the most careful defining of her sphere, and to that traditional sphere she must be held by the powerful constraint of public sentiment. With all our gallantry we have treated woman shabbily.

—William Xavier Ninde, Methodist Episcopal bishop
Chicago Training School address, ca. 1890

For many years the West has found it very convenient and quite to its own interest to regard the Orient as a sleeping giant which could be exploited or insulted as the occasion seemed to demand. It has been assumed that the white man, because of his superior intelligence and culture, has the first right to all the desirable places in the world; that men of color should do the bidding of the white man and contribute to his prosperity; that our self-imposed task of uplifting these backward races should atone for any seeming wrong and injustice that we may cause them to suffer.

—Jesse Frederick Steiner
The Japanese Invasion, 1917

. . . though I am not splenetive and rash,
Yet have I in me something dangerous . . .

—William Shakespeare, *Hamlet*

In the 1909 yearbook of Ohio Wesleyan University, a picture of a Japanese woman, identified as "Mae Russel" [*sic*], appears among the juniors' photographs. Each of the photographs is graced by a quote, many of them sensible ("The price of wisdom is above rubies," quotes one Nelle Rubey), but May Russell's chosen phrase, like her image, stands out from the others. Capturing the unsettling, mad wisdom of Hamlet, she quotes: "Though I am not splenetive and rash,/ Yet have I something in me, dangerous."

This young woman had been pushing Victorian boundaries her entire life. In 1885, three days after her birth, she was given to an unmarried, forty-eight-year-old American missionary woman in Japan, who named her Ellen May Russell and called her May. Although it is not clear if May was formally adopted, the missionary woman she knew as her mother, Elizabeth Russell, was determined to give her an identity as an American girl. May was sent to the United States at age eleven to prepare for American high school and college, during a time when xenophobia toward "Asiatics" was becoming stronger than ever there and Japanese were rejecting American imperialism. In a time when race and national identity were promoted as fixed, unchanging categories by the rising empires of both the United States and Japan, May's life reflected a more complex reality created by international communities in both the East and the West.

In addition to handing her this complicated national/ethnic identity, her mother also offered an unconventional road map for negotiating her identity as a woman, in a time when challenging prescribed gender roles was met with hostility in both Japan and the United States. Raised communally the first years of her life by unmarried American and Japanese women at a mission school founded by her mother in Nagasaki, she absorbed the conviction that a life in service to God and to womanhood was more valuable than fulfilling the Victorian ideals of marriage, motherhood, and domestic bliss. May followed the path of her mother(s), returning to Nagasaki after her graduation from Ohio Wesleyan University to teach in the mission school there. May and Elizabeth Russell remained close until May's death from tuberculosis at the age of thirty-nine, four years before Elizabeth died at the age of ninety-one.

May Russell was, in many ways, a product of the foreign mission movement of American women, which was able to reach Japan in the

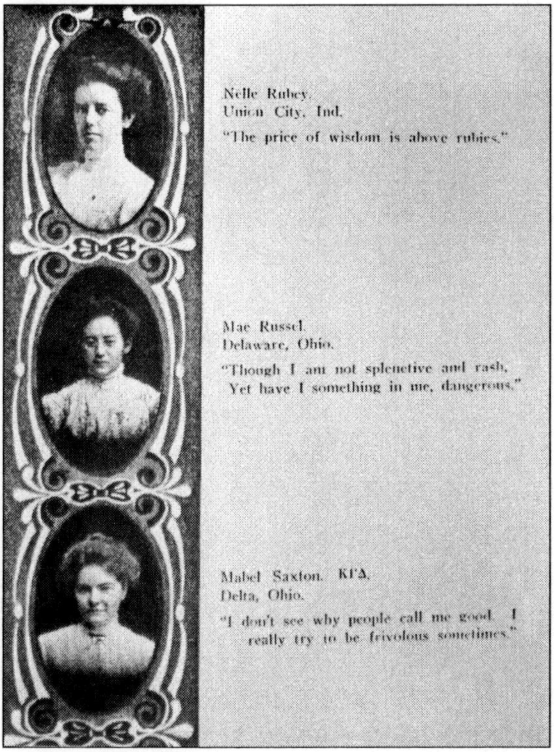

May Russell's Junior picture in the Ohio Wesleyan University Yearbook (Le Bijou), 1909. Housed at the Ohio Wesleyan University Historical Collection in Beeghly Library. Courtesy of Ohio Wesleyan University.

late nineteenth century as a result of American imperialism in the Pacific. While she apparently conformed to the mission movement's goal of godly service—seemingly harmless to American gender ideals and imperialist agendas—she also reflected the ways in which the American women's foreign mission movement undermined the very ideals that forged it. Missionaries often seemed to uphold American notions of civilization and race, yet they perpetually crossed and challenged national and ethnic boundaries. They claimed to promote the Victorian ideals of domestic womanhood, yet they relied on unmarried women to lead very public lives in bringing this message of uplift to their "sisters" around the world. These contradictions profoundly shaped May's life, and May seems to have understood on some level that her very identity represented the dangers inherent in the movement—the dangers of challenging dominant national, racial, and gender ideologies.

May was born in an age when, as indicated in the epigraphs by Bishop Ninde and Jesse Steiner, the "woman question" and the "race question" were on the minds of many in the United States and around the world. As a result of the "age of empire"[1]—and its attendant industrial, economic, and political upheavals—the worlds of men and women of all classes were rapidly changing. Global migration, including mass immigration to the United States, made it more difficult to identify what true manhood and womanhood *was,* as more and more people who looked and acted differently from each other came to live within the same national boundaries.

For many, the extent to which traditional concepts of womanhood were altered indicated the degree to which humanity had fallen away from the laws of God and nature—and many feared some "frightful cataclysm" might occur as a result, as the more liberal Bishop Ninde sardonically pointed out (Hughey [1891] 1987, 42). In a sense, changes in women's roles, rights, and identities did represent a danger to the foundations of many nineteenth-century societies—not only could these changes challenge the unquestioned rule of men but also the fundamental ideological bases of cultures, enshrined in centuries-old religious interpretation and sacred custom. Nineteenth-century women were indeed dangerous, as they continuously transgressed gender boundaries.

Conservative American ideologies of womanhood, in fact, were powerfully undermined by the very women who were charged to promote them—namely, white Protestant missionary women. While nineteenth-century missionaries were often the purveyors of what amounted to sexist and racist ideologies compatible with the age of imperialism, the mission movement was much more complicated and much less predictable than any such one-dimensional depiction. Ultimately, cross-cultural interactions made possible through missions helped to reshape American

1. This phrase references E. J. Hobsbawm's *The Age of Empire, 1875–1914.* Hobsbawm states that "the era from 1875 to 1914 may be called the Age of Empire. . . . most of the world outside Europe and the Americas was formally partitioned into territories under the formal rule or informal political domination of one or other of a handful of states: mainly Great Britain, France, Germany, Italy, the Netherlands, Belgium, the U.S.A. and Japan" (1987, 56–57).

understandings of gender and race. Missionaries' very appropriation of conservative ideologies actually made them more effective agents of change. Because of missionaries' often traditional rhetoric, the Protestant mainstream assumed that missionaries shared their values and saw them as a reliable source of information about the larger world. American Protestant women and men were just as likely, if not more likely, to listen to the missionaries they financed overseas than secular news sources. Church visits by missionaries on furlough and widely popular mission publications, to which missionaries contributed articles about their experiences in non-Western lands, exposed ordinary American Protestants to new ideas and a more global world view. Protestant missions, then, were an important influence on American culture in the late nineteenth and early twentieth centuries. This dynamic can be seen through the story of the Woman's Foreign Missionary Society (WFMS) of the Methodist Episcopal Church, an organization that brought unmarried women such as Elizabeth Russell out of America and into international settings, and also brought the overseas experiences of women like her into the homes of ordinary Americans through faithfully distributed missionary publications.

Protestant Gender Ideologies and Missions

Many Protestants in the late nineteenth century came to believe that women—both missionaries and converts—were key to Christianizing the world successfully. In the latter half of the nineteenth century, many more Protestant women than men became involved in the American mission movement, and women in almost every major Protestant denomination organized their own missionary societies. These woman-run mission organizations were highly successful in promoting their cause. Collectively, the women's mission movement was among the largest of the nineteenth-century American women's movements, and, arguably, the largest nineteenth-century religious movement in America (Hill 1985, 23).

Part of the success of women's missions was a result of the nineteenth-century Protestant belief that the creation and maintenance of a "Christian home"—where godliness and virtue were instilled and nourished by wives and mothers—was at the core of any civilization's strength. Even as gender roles were evolving in the United States and around the globe, many Protestants insisted that a properly gendered society was the key to God's favor.

The gender ideals at the foundation of the women's mission movement had taken root in the antebellum United States, as Americans imagined the proper role for women to play in a republic. Nineteenth-century Americans often described women and men as occupying "separate spheres"—physically, spiritually, mentally, spatially. Virtue, untainted by economic or political concerns, was a woman's special domain, as Barbara Welter so well describes in the now classic 1966 article "The Cult of True Womanhood, 1820–1860": "Religion or piety was the core of woman's virtue, the source of her strength. . . . This 'peculiar susceptibility' to religion was given her for a reason: 'the vestal flame of piety, lighted up by Heaven in the breast of woman' would throw its beams into the naughty world of men" (152).

This "separate spheres" ideal reflected the dominant gender *ideology* of the era, rather than a monolithic historical reality. Even though many nineteenth-century men and women, especially of the middle class, believed that the sexes ought to occupy separate spheres, this was not, of course, a universal reality for American women. Nancy Hoffman points out that

> there is substantial evidence that the match between the doctrine of separate spheres and material reality was "overly simple." From the turn of the eighteenth century on, women were increasing their participation in the market economy. . . . Prosperous women who led antebellum benevolent societies were often compensated for their work, and certainly carried out business-like practices. . . . In short, market and home interpenetrated, and gender identities were far more fluid than the metaphor of separate spheres would lead one to imagine. (2003, 32)

While the "separate spheres" ideology was becoming deeply embedded in the popular consciousness of the United States, women's movements arose, including the women's mission movement itself, that subtly subverted this ideal, both intentionally and unintentionally. In fact, by the late nineteenth century, thousands of American women involved in missions and other religious movements (most nineteenth-century reform movements were, in essence, religious) had neatly stepped outside their assigned role as domestic nurturer. With the conviction that God was on their side, American women, compelled by both religious fervor and market forces, helped to reshape American notions about separate spheres. The postbellum rise of vast and powerful organizations created by and for women, such as the politically active Woman's Christian Temperance Union and a host of independent women's missionary societies promoting unmarried women's public leadership, reveals that by the late nineteenth century "woman's sphere" was becoming much broader than the private space of the home.

Although the women who first organized independent missionary societies found it expedient to appropriate familiar language about gender in order to garner support for their cause, as was always the case in building independent women's organizations in the nineteenth century, the women's mission movement was in actuality comprised of women with a range of ideas about women's proper place and role in society. Missions attracted progressive women who sought a wider sphere of experience and influence for themselves and their sex, as well as women who were committed to replicating traditional American gender ideologies worldwide—and women who were motivated by elements from both of these agendas.

Women's missionary societies began their work in countries around the world with enthusiastic proclamations that the key to converting societies to Christianity and civilization was the conversion of women, who would then replicate the values of middle-class American Protestants in raising future generations. However, missionary organizations such as the Woman's Foreign Missionary Society of the Methodist Episcopal Church enacted policies and strategies that challenged their own focus on domesticity and motherhood. For pragmatic purposes, the WFMS sent only unmarried women, unhampered by their own domestic responsibilities, into the mission field. Moreover, the WFMS found that it was necessary to bring "heathen" women out into the public sphere to some extent, such as through the formation of women's schools, in order to have access to their souls.

Although early missionary rhetoric indicated that educational institutions for women should be viewed only as a means of converting non-Christian women, when highly educated unmarried American missionary women such as Elizabeth Russell became the norm in missions, alternative agendas were introduced into the program. Russell, and other missionary women like her, wanted to do more than convert Japanese women to Christianity. Russell, who was a product of the women's higher education movement in the United States, sought to provide non-Western women with the opportunities she herself had received: an education equal to that of men's education, and economic independence through a meaningful career.

These diverse agendas reflected larger divisions within nineteenth-century American Protestant culture. Even though Protestant literature often fixated on the domestic ideal for women and depicted gender as fixed and unchanging, in reality late-nineteenth-century Protestant denominations were often engaged in heated debates over women's religious, social, and legal rights. In the Methodist Episcopal Church, for example, support for women's rights within church, society, and civil government grew steadily throughout the nineteenth century, so much so that the 1880s and 1890s saw intense intradenominational debates over women's participation in traditionally male-dominated spheres, with much ink spilled over the woman question (see, for example, Gifford 1987).

The foreign mission fields served as a testing ground where women could experiment with new roles and implement new visions for womanhood, eventually influencing debates over women's rights back in the United States. Through their experiences in the field, many missionary women, over time, began questioning whether women around the world might be better off with job training, voting rights, and even independence from racist/imperialist influences, rather than traditional Protestant ideals of domesticity. As missionaries' evolving world views were published in widely circulated mission magazines, these new ideas reached the homes of Protestant women throughout the United States, with an influence that no other source could have had. Thus, even while the American women's mission movement appropriated conservative gender ideologies, it also challenged American Protestants to reexamine their views on women and their understandings of the wider world. Beginning as a movement to bring Protestants' domestic ideal to women around the globe, the women's mission movement ultimately challenged the notion that women's proper place was in the home, and that all the world should replicate white Anglo-Saxon Protestant American values.

By 1910, Helen Barrett Montgomery, a well-respected missions scholar of her day, identified the women's mission movement not as the bulwark of traditional gender ideologies but as one of the major forces behind the subversion and rejection of the ideology of True Womanhood. In her seminal work *Western Women in Eastern Lands,* she stated, "The organization of the Women's Missionary Societies is but one of a remarkable series of movements among women that have made the nineteenth century known as the Woman's Century. In it forces long at work crystallized so as to revolutionize many conceptions regarding the proper sphere and activities of women" (1910, 3).

Certainly, the transformation of the ideology of True Womanhood in American Protestant circles was not a sudden occurrence but a shift that happened over decades by those who were deeply committed to traditional gender ideals. Ironically, by embracing parts of the ideology of True Womanhood, women involved in religious and reform work more easily stepped outside their traditional roles. And it was such women, who were more embedded in conservative circles than open advocates of women's rights, who subtly shifted mainstream American Protestant ideals of womanhood. Women involved in missions played an important role in influencing white, middle-class Protestants—the most culturally and politically powerful American population of the era—to be more comfortable with women's growing rights and responsibilities.

American Missions in Japan

Largely because the women's foreign mission movement sent American women to work in every country open to them, as Amanda Porterfield has stated, "American influence in the nonwestern world has been shaped more by women and women's issues than many historians have realized" (1997, 7). Missionary women opened schools for girls and women around the world, and struggled to develop "appropriate" curricula for women in their particular cultural contexts. This activity led missionaries to become involved in local controversies about the woman question, as the communities with which missionaries engaged faced ever-shifting economic and social conditions at the end of the nineteenth century. Negotiating such controversies was part of the process by which missionary women began to reexamine, and often alter, their own assumptions about gender and race. This dynamic was dramatically played out in Japan, as the Meiji government (1868–1912) sought to reshape the Japanese educational system, initially in response to the United States' imperialist interventions.

At the end of the nineteenth century, Japan held both a special promise and an unique threat to American Protestants. Japan opened its doors to Christian missions and adopted Western-style institutions and industries, fostering missionaries' hopes that it was to be the "gateway" to Christianizing Asia. Since it was one of the only non-Western countries of the day that was not formally colonized, missionaries believed Japan held the potential to show the world what Christianity and Western civilization, voluntarily adopted by Japanese families, could do to transform a country into a free and successful land almost as good as the United States itself.

However, Japan's relatively independent political status posed unprecedented problems for American missionaries. It turned out not to be so easy to transport American Protestant cultural ideals, especially when the government was not particularly invested in their Christianizing project and ultimately became quite hostile to it. Historically, Western colonialism was, for the most part, what made sustained foreign missions possible. The existence of a Western ruling power in a non-Western culture increased the odds that missionaries would achieve their goals in developing and maintaining Christian institutions overseas. While American missionaries in the nineteenth century usually gained access to territories controlled by Western powers, such as British India or the Belgian Congo, an independent country such as Japan posed unique problems. While Japanese leaders accepted missionaries into the country as part of their efforts to ward off more direct Western imperialism, missionaries were required to negotiate with a non-Western and non-Christian government on its own terms.

American missionary work in Japan began soon after Commodore Matthew Perry's 1853 expedition to the "island nation"—one of the major events of the nineteenth century signaling a new age in global commerce. Commodore Perry's U.S. Navy fleet brought an ultimatum for the relatively secluded country to open up economic relations with the United States or risk invasion and war. Perry's encounter with Japan helped secure the United States' new status as a growing world power. Having just recently expanded its territory across the Americas to the Pacific Ocean, the United States was now becoming an imperialist force overseas.

On the one hand, Protestant missions legitimated the United States' expansionist project. In spite of the social upheavals related to American expansion—industrialization and urbanization often vexed Protestants throughout the nineteenth century—many Protestants believed in the potential of modern progress to be a blessing, so long as modernizing countries followed God's mandates. Many Protestants understood the United States' global power in terms of God's plan for human history and believed God had made the United States powerful as a way of spreading Christianity to the "dark corners" of the earth. As the U.S. government began to expand its sphere of influence across the Pacific Ocean, so did U.S. religious institutions, with the belief that God was guiding the whole project in order to bring "all the nations under His fold."

On the other hand, Protestant missionaries' goals were not identical with the political and economic goals of the expansionist United States. While many in the United States and other imperialist nations merely sought to control and exploit resources around the world, missionaries, overall, truly desired—albeit with frequent insensitivity—to help people in non-Western cultures attain the success they believed the United States had achieved because of its Christian character. While this was an ethnocentric view, it was not identical to the view of pure capitalist interests. Missionaries were just as likely to criticize U.S. imperialism as support it, if they became convinced that U.S. government and business interests were not fostering the Christianization of the world.

Missionaries believed the United States' move to open Japan to the West was very good news for the spread of Christianity; thus the displeasure of numerous Japanese over U.S. intervention had little impact on nineteenth-century missionaries' enthusiasm about newly forged U.S.-Japan relations. Soon after receiving the ultimatum from Perry, Japanese leaders succumbed to the pressure, and in the 1850s they signed treaties with the United States and other Western powers, which came to be known, from the Japanese perspective, as the "Unequal Treaties." This brought the already-existing political turmoil in Japan to a head; in the following decade the feudal-style government of Japan was overthrown by disaffected samurai, and the Meiji period (1868–1912) began. Initially, the Meiji government adopted a policy of appropriating certain Western institutions and ideologies—such as those related to business, government, and education—as the most viable means of staving off Western imperialism and securing revised treaties. As a result, American missionaries had opportunities to develop numerous educational institutions and serve in a variety of advisory capacities in Japan during the early years of the Meiji period, and American missionaries were active participants in the reconstruction of Japan. In a period of less than fifty years, Japan changed from a relatively secluded, agrarian, and fragmented country to become a unified, industrialized, and imperialist nation-state governed by a constitutional monarchy. As the Japanese government became more powerful, however, missionaries' activities were increasingly regulated.

The Meiji period coincided with the rise of the women's foreign mission movement in the United States. Thus it provided an unprecedented opportunity for women's missions to participate in a new mission field from the beginning. Their focus on women's education originally helped establish American women's missions in Japan, but ultimately it led to conflicts with the Japanese government. As the Japanese government worked on securing a competitive position among the world's powers, Japanese officials developed their own agendas for Japanese families and promoted gender ideologies that did not always resonate with Protestant missionaries' ideals.

After a tenuous initiation upon the arrival of American women missionaries in the 1870s, mission schools for girls and women in Japan achieved great success by the 1880s. In 1872 Japanese officials decreed that all Japanese citizens should receive a primary education, regardless of gender or class, yet the government failed to follow through with adequate educational accommodations, especially for girls. When Japan's ban on Christianity was lifted in 1873, missionaries rushed to fill Japan's educational void. The first mission schools faced Japan's long history of anti-Christian sentiment, and although they were valued by the government for the inexpensive education they offered, many Japanese were suspicious of the religious ideologies of the missionary faculty. As the government continued to promote its pro-Westernization strategy, however, mission schools—particularly schools for women—eventually became quite popular, and in the 1880s missionary reports frequently referenced rapidly growing enrollments and "crowded quarters" in their schools. Missionaries mistakenly believed Christianity would be adopted by Japan as enthusiastically as the country seemed to be embracing Western-style education.

To the dismay of missionaries, Japan's political climate reversed sharply in the late 1880s and 1890s. As confidence in Japan's success as a national power grew, reactions against borrowing from the West developed. When Japanese women became involved in antigovernment protest movements, for example, the government blamed this on the corrupting influence of Western thought, and Christianity and women's education (both identified with the West) became closely associated with political dissent in officials' minds. Women's mission schools came under fire, harshly criticized by government officials for failing to properly educate women. Many private Christian schools for women were thrown into crisis in the 1890s as the government mandated that each prefecture provide a public postprimary girls' school focused on creating patriotic wives and mothers, and opposed schools that represented alternate ideologies, including schools with overtly Christian activities or curricula that were perceived to be too similar to men's education. Over the course of the Meiji period, discourses on gender in Japan increasingly naturalized women's obedience and exclusion from direct participation in politics. Thus, by the end of the nineteenth century, as Japan had become a miracle example of progress and modernity, Japanese women found themselves systematically disempowered, as the lives of women were carefully regulated to fit government agendas. Mission schools were compelled to rethink their methods for maintaining enrollments in this new environment and forced to recognize that they did not have as much control in shaping the country as they had earlier believed.

Missionary Women Negotiate the Japanese Context

Records of missionary women's writings and activities reveal their struggle in negotiating the often-contradictory ideologies they encountered through their position in Japan. Using the ideology of domesticity to support their public activities connected to the expansion of Western civilization, missionary women were caught between their admiration of and revulsion to the observed roles of women in Japan. While they frequently praised the behavior and character of Japanese women—which they often stated was closer to the ideal of True Womanhood than the behavior and character of American women—missionary women, who themselves were uniquely ambitious and career-oriented for their day, were also repelled by the apparent low status of women in Japan. Influenced by their imperialist homeland's ethnocentricity, as well as reform-minded American women's concern with the status of women around the globe, missionary women were torn between prevailing Western rhetoric that Christianity and Westernization would improve the status of women worldwide, and their real-life experiences that gave rise to questions as to whether foreign education, and the process of modernization in general, was as beneficial to Japanese women as expected.

Missionary women had arrived in Japan determined to transform its culture through changing the domestic sphere. As they became more acculturated to their adopted country, however, they increasingly became nostalgic for the old Japan, which was disappearing before their eyes. Clara Whitney—the daughter of an American businessman in Meiji Japan—reflected the sentiments of many Western women in the country when she wrote in her diary, "Oh, this life in Japan: fascinating, yet repulsive, lovely, yet full of despair to me" (1979, 104). While Margaret Burton, in *The Education of Women in Japan,* argued that mission schools were important for "the development of strong, efficient Christian women, able to guide the bewildered womanhood of Japan through this time of transition," she also worried that "the complaint that [mission schools'] course of study resulted in the too great Westernization of their pupils was probably not entirely unfounded," and she took note of critiques that mission schools would "destroy the beautiful ideals of Japanese womanhood" (1914, 228, 68–69, 72).

Nevertheless, Burton urged women involved in education in Japan to resist the notion that Japanese women could not receive new levels of education without completely losing their cultural heritage. Japanese women were the ones, after all, who were ultimately choosing new paths of education and public activity, while deciding which aspects of their heritage continued to have value. Burton highlighted the words of prominent Japanese educator Naruse Jinzō, who, unlike conservatives who criticized women's modern education, supported programs that made young women "more independent in their spirit"; he asserted that "conflict between the old ideas and the new in such a period of transition as our country had undergone could not possibly be avoided" (1914, 71). When encountering opposition to their work, missionaries who promoted women's education in Japan also took comfort in remembering how American women had overcome similar opposition to women's education in the United States only decades earlier. However, Japanese conflicts over women's roles were even more complicated than in the United States, in that social changes in Japan at this time were largely fueled by the external intervention of the West, making shifts in women's roles seem foreign to critics, in addition to unnatural.

Conflict over women's education not only existed between traditionalists and modernists in Japanese circles, but among missionaries as well. The challenge of meeting governmental expectations for women's education in Japan exacerbated the already-existing ideological splits among Protestant women missionaries. Some mission schools opted to side with elements of the Japanese government's agenda for women. Moving away from the original ideals of creating American-style True Women, these schools, in an attempt to stay in the good graces of their host country, focused on such things as noncontroversial Japanese traditional arts for women. They argued that overeducating Japanese women was doing them no favor, for in so doing they were creating misfits, "square pegs for round holes," by "educating their students 'out of their sphere'" (Burton 1914, 70).

However, other mission schools, such as Elizabeth Russell's Kwassui Jo Gakkō, responded to challenges from the Japanese government in quite the opposite manner. Although Russell's school added courses to appease both Japanese and missionary conservatives, it continuously expanded programs of higher education, even in the face of criticism. Missionary women such as Russell were often at odds with both government gender ideologies as well as the mission movement's original ideals and strategies.

Yet her mission school was extraordinarily successful in weathering the political tides of Meiji-era Japan.

It is crucial to highlight that what families wanted for their daughters, and what young women themselves wanted, figured significantly in the ongoing debates concerning women's education. While certain mission schools shrank from the criticisms that they were producing overly educated women who had lost their femininity and "walked like men" (Rose 1992, 50), Russell persisted in providing her students with a level of education equal to that of men's higher education in Japan and the United States. Japanese resisted government regulations by enrolling their daughters and/or themselves in mission schools such as Russell's, rather than cooperating with the government's new program of higher education for women that focused on domestic sciences and patriotism. The reality that a significant number of Japanese desired higher education for women became clearer than ever when several private Japanese colleges for women were opened in the first years of the twentieth century, including Japan Women's College *(Nihon Joshi Daigaku)*, founded in 1901 by Naruse Jinzō. Women who graduated from Elizabeth Russell's own Kwassui were known for choosing careers unusual for their gender, as a number of graduates became professionals in areas such as medicine and business. They were among the small but influential class of women who began to change popular perceptions of womanhood as Japan entered the twentieth century.

By the beginning of the twentieth century, most missionaries in Japan embraced strategies similar to Russell's and openly advocated women's higher education as the key for keeping mission schools for Japanese women marketable. The original goal of preparing women to be Christian wives and mothers was eventually overshadowed by the need to compete with Japanese schools in attracting students, and as a result more progressive missionary women's agendas started to be widely adopted as general mission strategy. Regardless of the varying levels of ethnocentrism displayed by missionary faculty and administrators, Japanese women made use of the opportunities provided by mission schools. Although having been uneven in the level of education they provided before 1899, these institutions, along with a handful of private Japanese schools, came to function as one of the few spaces where women in Japan could find "intellectual challenges and a humanistic view of women" (Sievers 1983, 104).

Missionaries' Influence in the United States

By the twentieth century, many missionaries involved in Japan came to embrace liberal values resonating with the more progressive wings of American Protestantism. Chastened by the Japanese government's growing power over their activities, and transformed by their daily experiences with exceptional Japanese women who sought higher education at their schools, missionary women began to champion ideals of ethnic and gender equality, and they worked to change Americans' perceptions of gender and ethnicity back home. Missionaries were a major source of information about Japan for Americans, and they consistently opposed growing anti-Japanese hysteria in the United States. In article after article about women's mission work in Japan, mission publications distributed a sympathetic view of the country; one piece about missionaries in Hokkaidō (Japan's northern island), so enthusiastic about "the Christian training and culture of the new womanhood of Japan," stated of the missionaries: "How loyal they are to Japan—North Japan, Banzai!" Missionaries often saw themselves as the antidote to racism, because instead of accepting widely popular notions of racial differences during the high age of imperialism, they persistently sought to erase racial and cultural differences through a universal Christianity. That this was yet another kind of ethnocentric, even imperialist, project did not occur to them. Nevertheless, for many missionaries, especially in Japan, the sharp edges of their own ethnocentrism became muted over time. They often moved away from the mainstream perspectives of American Protestant culture, becoming increasingly integrated into their new host country. As one missionary stated, "distinctions of country and race are forgotten . . . where underneath love of fatherland and people burns an intenser love for the kingdom that is not of this earth" (WFMS, *WMF*, 1905, 37, no. 6:192).

Moreover, women's missionary literature, as it hailed the successes of women missionary professionals and women's education in Japan, continuously placed a progressive vision of womanhood into the hands of an

American Protestant public. As women became more confident through their successes in the mission field, they began to more closely reflect the goals of women's rights supporters. As historian Patricia Hill states in her discussion of Estelle Freedman's article on nineteenth-century women's institution building, while women "drew upon the ideology of true womanhood with its concept of female moral superiority to create separate female associations that provided them with opportunities to pursue careers. . . . [the] women who built such separate institutions frequently abandoned the ideology that had empowered them" (Hill 1985, 117). Ultimately, as Freedman notes, as they "entered a public female world, they adopted the more radical stance of feminists" (Freedman 1979, 521; qtd. in Hill 1985, 117). By the early twentieth century, influential leaders of the American women's mission movement openly supported the women's suffrage movement, something the founders of the mission movement never would have considered.

Such shifts in the women's mission movement reveal that through global expansionism the Western world was itself reshaped, as was the non-Western world. Americans' engagement with non-Western countries—such as that of American missionary women in Japan—gave rise to new ways of thinking and self-understanding within the imperialist culture itself.

2

"Translated from Darkness to Light"

The Formation of an American Missionary Woman

> Secure I rest upon the wave,
> For thou, O Lord! Hast power to save.
> I know thou wilt not slight my call. . . .
>
> —Emma Willard, "Rocked in the Cradle of the Deep"

The life of Elizabeth Russell (1836–1928) illustrates the expanding possibilities available to white, middle-class American women in the latter half of the nineteenth century, as the United States became a major player on the world stage. Born on October 9, 1836, Russell would inhabit a number of identities available to women of her generation: student, spinster, teacher, invalid, mother, and, finally, missionary extraordinaire.[1] During her forty-year career as a missionary to Japan, she promoted progressive ideas about women's education and social roles, both through the example

1. Sources directly relating to Elizabeth Russell's life can be found in the Russell Collection at Kwassui Women's College in Nagasaki, Japan. The sources in this collection include Russell's personal journal (the original and a transcription), Russell's personal correspondence, census records, and travel documents. The collection also holds an unpublished article by retired Kwassui teacher Patricia McCreary, "Realms of Glory: The Life of Elizabeth Russell" (1992), which was informed by interviews with the descendants of Russell's nieces and nephews. Additionally, items written by and about Russell can be found in Methodist Episcopal mission publications.

of her own life and through her writings disseminated by the Woman's Foreign Missionary Society of the Methodist Episcopal Church.

Born to a family of modest income, Russell was fortunate to receive a relatively advanced education for a woman of her generation.[2] Like her contemporaries, Russell's life was profoundly shaped by continuous and dramatic change brought by rapid industrialization, war, and the constant proximity of death. She most certainly would not have viewed the world as a static place.

She was raised in the rapidly growing river town of Wheeling, Virginia (later West Virginia), where her father, John W. Russell, had found opportunity in 1842 working as a millwright for Hamilton & Clark Machine Works, which produced machinery for the coal-mining industry. Elizabeth and her family saw their world expand as the first suspension bridge over the Ohio River at Wheeling was completed in 1849, and as the Baltimore & Ohio Railroad reached Wheeling in 1852, making the city a major industrial center of the region and a magnet for new immigrants (Fones-Wolf and Lewis 2002). Elizabeth grew up in a time when industrial, economic, and social conditions throughout the United States were undergoing radical transformations; technological innovations led to mass production and mobility like never before. Such developments were part of the industrial revolution, which in the United States and beyond, as Peter N. Stearns states, "[had] ramifications reaching into almost every aspect of human experience—into the habits of thought and the relations between men and women as well as into systems of production and exchange" (1998, 5).

Born in 1809 to an Irish immigrant and the daughter of a Revolutionary War veteran, John W. Russell spent his prime working years following new opportunities in industry, moving his family from their home state of Pennsylvania to Cadiz, Ohio (where Elizabeth was born), and then to Wheeling. Elizabeth's mother, Julia Ann Russell (b. ca. 1811), followed patterns that were both similar and dissimilar to generations of women before her. Mirroring the lives of her agrarian ancestors, Julia Ann spent most

2. As historian Jane Hunter states, most Protestant women who became missionaries in the nineteenth century were from relatively humble middle-class backgrounds (1984, 28–30).

of her adult life bearing children; she bore her first child eight months after her marriage in 1834, proceeded to bear a child every two to three years for the next eleven years, and died in her forties in 1855.[3] Nevertheless, one can presume that the industrial revolution affected her as well. Little is recorded of Julia Ann's life—virtually nothing of her world view or daily activities other than childcare—but with a husband working in industry and living in a booming city at midcentury, she most likely had a different set of expectations and activities than her foremothers. The meaning of the home had begun to be understood in new ways, as U.S. economic production was shifting its primary center away from the home and farm and into the factories. Although, as Stearns notes, "remnants of older domestic activity persisted into the twentieth century" and families "retained a host of economic functions" (1998, 61),[4] in the minds of many middle-class Americans in urbanizing areas, the home was now a sphere of reproduction, rather than production, where women would raise future generations of good citizens and laborers. The private sphere of the home, according to the new domestic ideal of the nineteenth century, was a place for nurture and spirituality, which would function as a haven for men, who worked in the rational, political, crass, and industrializing public sphere.[5] While this ideal did not adequately reflect the reality of the scores

3. Elizabeth Russell's personal journal references the date of her mother's death. Perhaps with the intention of creating a memoir, Russell wrote this journal toward the end of her life, with accounts of her childhood memories and detailed descriptions of events throughout her career.

4. Like Stearns, Jeanne Boydston (1990) and others have shown that women of this era were involved in domestic labor that was of great economic importance to the industrializing United States, although their domestic work was devalued and even made invisible through newly developing capitalist ideologies and gender ideologies.

5. Nancy Cott, in *The Bonds of Womanhood: "Women's Sphere" in New England, 1780–1835*, reveals how the domestic ideal was imagined by its advocates in the words of one New Hampshire pastor, who in 1827 stated, "It is at home, where man . . . seeks a refuge from the vexations and embarrassments of business, an enchanting repose from exertion, a relaxation from care by the interchange of affection: where some of his finest sympathies, tastes, and moral religious feelings are formed and nourished;—where is the treasury of pure disinterested love, such as is seldom found in the busy walks of a selfish and calculating world" (1977, 64).

of poor, working, and/or enslaved women in the United States at this time, Julia Ann lived up to this ideal in ways that would have been considered respectable for a woman of her day. She followed her husband to the city where he found work and made a home for him and their six children, all of whom, except for a son who died as a young child, became apparently successful and religiously devout adults (McCreary 1992).

Julia Ann's two daughters, Elizabeth and Julia Texanna (who later, perhaps not surprisingly, changed her name to Julia Ann), revealed in their life choices a wider spectrum of possible roles for women living in the nineteenth century. At one end of the spectrum, daughter Julia (b. 1838) followed the most idealized path for a nineteenth-century woman; like her mother, she married and spent her prime years bearing children. At the other end of the spectrum, Elizabeth followed paths newly available to women and pursued higher education and a career. Like numerous women who were of marriageable age during the Civil War, when young men were slaughtered by the tens of thousands, Elizabeth never married. And, like many exceptionally ambitious women of the day, she did not express regret over her marital status. Instead, she craved education, independence, and a position of influence, all of which she eventually achieved over the course of her life.

Elizabeth was able to realize her goals, first because of the nineteenth-century movement for women's education, which had begun not long before her birth, and secondly because of the women's foreign mission movement, which carried new standards for female education around the world. The rise of women's higher education in the nineteenth century is a prime example of a movement that both reinforced the "Cult of True Womanhood"[6] and subverted it. Like that of thousands of other women, Elizabeth Russell's life was profoundly influenced by the formidable and famous leaders of the women's education movement—most notably Emma Hart Willard (1787–1870), Mary Lyon (1797–1849), and Catharine Beecher (1800–1878), all of whom used the prevailing gender ideologies of the early

6. A term used to describe the nineteenth-century gender ideology of separate spheres, from Welter's article "The Cult of True Womanhood, 1820–1860" (1966).

republic to forge new opportunities for women. Emma Willard, in fact, had a quite direct impact on Elizabeth Russell's life, as she was the teacher, mentor, and friend of Elizabeth's own mentor, Sarah Foster Hanna.

Socially minded women such as Willard, Lyon, and Beecher sought to increase the value placed on women by the popular consciousness of their day, while complexly and ambivalently appropriating the prevailing ideology that placed women and the private sphere outside the realm of politics and economics. At times all three of these very public women encouraged others of their sex to accept their domestic role, even within a democratic society that valued the discourse of equal rights. The twist they put on the separate spheres ideal, however, was that they insisted the domestic sphere was in fact at the core of civil society, and therefore the women who occupied this sphere were the nation's most precious resource.

Catharine Beecher, in particular, was most famous for increasing the status of women's prescribed role in society instead of completely rejecting it. Beecher cemented the domestic ideal in the minds of Americans when she published *A Treatise on Domestic Economy* in 1841. Arguing that women's moral power in the domestic sphere was *more* important than direct political power in the public sphere, Beecher's *Treatise* resonated with the American public, going through multiple reprintings in the following two decades (Sklar 1973, 151). Beecher, as well as Lyon and Willard, stressed that the republic could not progress without a strong, moral, Christian core, and it was women who provided that foundation. Women were the ones who molded future generations and who provided a moral anchor for their husbands. As more and more Americans came to embrace this view of women's role in society, Beecher, Lyon, and Willard were able to build a logic for women's education. Beecher stated:

> The mother writes the character of the future man; the sister bends the fibres that hereafter are the forest tree; the wife sways the heart, whose energies may turn for good or for evil the destinies of a nation. Let the women of a country be made virtuous and intelligent, and the men will certainly be the same. The proper education of a man decides the welfare of an individual; but educate a woman, and the interests of a whole family are secured. (1841, 13)

Furthermore, Beecher, Lyon, and Willard argued that women in the United States not only had a responsibility to elevate their own nation but had a responsibility to elevate nations around the world. Asserting that the United States was called to be involved in "the destiny of the whole earth," Beecher stated that "to American women, more than to any others on earth, is committed the exalted privilege of extending over the world those blessed influences, that are to renovate degraded man, and 'clothe all climes with beauty'" (1841, 13). Such efforts to popularize their ideals for American womanhood, then, not only reinforced women's prescribed roles as wives and mothers, but also laid the foundation for the women's mission movement.

Mary Lyon's Mount Holyoke Female Seminary, from its inception in 1837, was particularly focused on training women to become missionaries. Many years later, an 1895 article in *The Heathen Woman's Friend,* a magazine of the Woman's Foreign Missionary Society of the Methodist Episcopal Church, emphasized the connection between women's education and the women's mission movement:

> At the beginning of the century barriers to the spread of the gospel among woman in darkened lands seemed impenetrable, but while they have been breaking away, the phenomenal educational movement . . . in the middle decades of the century . . . has in these last years furnished opportunity for women to adequately prepare themselves for this high vocation in all intellectual lines. . . .
>
> [T]he sun never sets upon a missionary from Mt. Holyoke College, and . . . almost every college has its representatives in foreign lands. (26, no. 12:341)

Emma Willard: Her Vision and Influence

Emma Willard was one of the first individuals to pioneer both higher education for women and the teaching profession itself in the United States. Willard organized a high-level female academy in 1814 and ultimately founded the famous Troy Female Seminary in 1821. She encouraged thousands of women to move into new, unchartered territories for their sex in academic and professional work.[7] Working tirelessly for over half a century to convince the world of women's intellectual abilities, she generated a network of progressive women's schools throughout the United States and beyond. Willard became a nationally recognized figure whose force of vision helped to establish teaching as a profession in its own right, and a profession to which women would have access. Creating a school that would produce female teachers in high demand in the growing field of education endowed Willard with a unique influence; it has been said that "Emma Willard's signature on a letter of recommendation was the first form of teacher certification in this country" (Scott 1979, 8).

Troy Female Seminary, in Troy, New York, was her mother ship. At Troy, Willard developed a school that rivaled the best men's colleges, while strategically using the popular rhetoric of the day: stressing separate spheres for men and women. Troy was one of the first female seminaries to offer women a curriculum including sciences, mathematics, and Latin—courses that gave distinction to men's colleges in the nineteenth century—and it set a precedent for other progressive female academies to follow, including the school Elizabeth Russell would one day establish in Japan.

Willard was inspired as a youth to undertake the project of improving women's education because, like Elizabeth Russell and countless other nineteenth-century women, "her soul panted for a wider sphere" (Lord 1873, 46; qtd. in Scott 1978, 687). In an effort to find government support for her endeavor to establish a female seminary, Willard proceeded to carve out a new space for herself and future women by writing a document titled *An Address to the Public, Particularly to the Members of the Legislature of New-York, Proposing a Plan for Improving Female Education* ([1819] 1987). She presented this plan to the New York legislature and widely circulated it among men of influence. Never one to set her sights too low, she even petitioned for support from the likes of John Adams, Thomas Jefferson, and the United States' president at the time of her publication, James Monroe. In her plan, Willard catered to her all-male audience by playing on their assumptions

7. For more complete treatments of Emma Willard's life and work, see Scott 1978 and 1979, Lutz 1929, and Lord 1873.

that any respectable person such as herself would support separate spheres for men and women; at the same time, however, she never acknowledged that women should be in a subordinate position to men. Even though she likely always intended to develop a college-level academy for women, she was able to get a hearing for her plan by stating at the beginning, "The idea of a college for males, will naturally be associated with that of a seminary, instituted and endowed by the public; and the absurdity of sending ladies to college, may, at first thought, strike every one to whom this subject shall be proposed. I therefore hasten to observe, that the seminary here recommended, will be as different from those appropriated to the other sex, as the female character and duties are from the male" ([1819] 1987, 7).

Willard made the point, to be repeated by countless advocates of female education, that educating women was important primarily because the "characters of [citizens] will be formed by their mothers; and it is through the mothers, that the government can control the characters of its future citizens, to form them such as will ensure their country's prosperity" ([1819] 1987, 18). She also strategically emphasized that female education would be in the best economic interest of the state by indicating that it would create a pool of easily exploitable female labor for schools—a point she "lived to regret," according to historian Anne Firor Scott (1978, 686). "There are many females of ability," Willard stated,

> to whom the business of instructing children is highly acceptable, and, who would devote all their faculties to their occupation. They would have no higher pecuniary object to engage their attention . . . whereas, whenever able and enterprising men, engage in this business, they consider it, merely as a temporary employment. . . . If then women were properly fitted by instruction, they would be likely to teach children better than the other sex; [and] they could afford to do it cheaper. ([1819] 1987, 30)

Willard also used more risky rhetoric indicating that it was wrong to consider women the subordinates of men. At one point in the plan, she waxed poetically: "Reason and religion teach, that we too are primary existencies; that it is for us to move, in the orbit of our duty, around the Holy Centre of perfection, the companions, not the satellites of men" ([1819]

1987, 17). With its combination of boldness and conservatism, Willard's plan did get her a charter for a female academy, if not an endowment, from the legislature (Scott 1978, 687).

Willard then proceeded to develop a school that offered an education well beyond her plan's proposed curriculum of religious, literary, domestic, and ornamental courses. While Willard may have sounded like an advocate of separate spheres in her plan, as she had made sure the legislature did not see the frightful "phantom of a college-learned lady" in her proposal ([1819] 1987, 19), she ultimately developed the very mode of education that she had acknowledged her audience might see as an absurdity—a college-level education for women. Developing intellectual abilities in people who would likely never be able to reap the full social and economic benefits of this training, as Willard did at Troy Seminary, was a direct challenge to the gender division of nineteenth-century America; even if this challenge was never openly acknowledged by Willard, actions spoke louder than words. It is no surprise that a number of women who successfully completed Willard's rigorous educational track began to question the limits placed on them in the larger society. The education provided by Troy Seminary and its offshoots gave women the tools to continue Emma Willard's work of carving out a wider sphere for women by finding innovative ways to use their skills and abilities.

Emma Willard's strong personality attracted women of similar temperament, and these women, in turn, went out to cultivate equally ambitious women. One of Willard's most famous students, women's suffrage leader Elizabeth Cady Stanton, described Willard as having "profound self-respect (a rare quality in woman) which gave her a dignity truly regal" (qtd. in Lutz 1929, 173). Willard's student and friend Sarah Foster (later Sarah Hanna), who would go on to become the principal of Washington Female Seminary for thirty-four years, was described, like Willard, as having a "commanding presence" and "great executive ability." She was also an impressive sight to behold, "always . . . gowned in lustrous black silk and a velvet cape. . . . [and wearing] a heavy gold watch chain" (Branton 1977, 7–8, 16). In turn, Foster's student Elizabeth Russell would one day be described by her missionary colleagues in Japan as having the presence and impact of a queen and even a bishop. It was this quality of great self-assurance, cultivated in women throughout Willard's network of schools, that likely helped many of them sidestep or silence the men and women who opposed their sometimes unconventional work for women.

Like the future founders of independent women's missionary societies, one reason Willard was able to take bold new steps for women was because she justified her activities with the familiar religious language of the day. Much of her confident energy, like that of her protégées, was inspired by the conviction that she was on a mission from God. As one admirer stated, Willard "was an apostle—an evangel of the higher education of women" (Fairbanks 1898, 24). Having received a divine call to improve women's education, Willard believed she was obliged to follow the will of God, rather than the expectations of the world. This was part and parcel of the fervent world view of evangelical Protestantism, the driving force behind the dominant culture of the United States. For those operating within the logic of evangelical America, it could be very difficult to argue with someone who had a call from God (especially if that person carried herself like a queen/mother). Moreover, if one was inclined to believe women were put on earth to shape the moral character of society, then it was not so hard to believe the logic put forth by these women of such impressive stature: that women should have access to institutions and organizations that would help them achieve this purpose. Many men of prominence—both impressed by Willard's competent piety and reassured by her claim that women's education was of no threat to their position of power—were quite willing to give some measure of support for her vision of female education. After many years of publicizing her vision, for example, the men of Kensington, Connecticut, literally gave her their vote of confidence when they elected her to the very public position of supervisor of the Kensington school system (Scott 1978, 700).

This is not to say that women who took these unconventional paths did not meet resistance and even ridicule; nor did they dare venture too far into men's sphere. Women's higher education advanced in part because the men who had the power to give or withdraw their support were convinced that women's education was in their best interest. A town with a female seminary established it as a place where cultured families (always a boon to a business community) could raise cultured daughters, find serious, level-headed wives for their sons, and train unmarried women for a respectable profession. A good female seminary could provide well-trained teachers willing to work for low pay in the rapidly expanding public school system (as Willard herself had so strategically pointed out in her plan), not only because of the limited employment opportunities for their sex, but also because, as educated women often insisted—no doubt to the delight of their supporters among the male economic elite—they had a higher calling than just crass economic gain.

Women reaching a high level of power and influence in the nineteenth century, like Willard and her protégées, felt the pressure to be very careful not to seem to have overstepped their bounds, and even the most careful woman could expect gossip about whether her motives were truly selfless. Willard was quite firm about following the social protocols of her day; for example, she made certain that she never made an address to an audience with men, at least technically (she would at times consent to speak to mixed audiences while sitting down, so that it could be called a conversation rather than a lecture). Despite her efforts at propriety, she spoke of "slanderous aspersions" that her work was motivated by a desire for fame rather than a higher calling (Scott 1978, 694). Elizabeth Russell would one day face similar accusations from the community of foreign settlers in Japan.

Willard's protégé and the direct mentor of Elizabeth Russell, Sarah Foster (who became Sarah Hanna in 1848, when at the age of forty-six she married the Reverend Dr. Thomas Hanna) was less inclined to follow social convention than Willard herself. Perhaps she had had her fill of convention as a young woman, when she spent many years longing for a higher education but was restrained by the objections of her mother. She was able to attend Troy Female Seminary only after the death of her mother in 1833, when Sarah was thirty-one, and her father allowed her to enroll in Troy. There she became a close friend of Willard's, and in 1836 Willard recommended her to Washington Female Seminary in Washington, Pennsylvania, when its board of trustees sought a female principal from among Troy's graduates.[8]

8. Foster, however, had already committed to another school and so did not secure the principalship of Washington Female Seminary until 1840.

Once at Washington Seminary, Foster was expected to submit to the authority of the school's all-male board of trustees, made up of the town's most prominent men—ministers, doctors, and lawyers all—but Foster, described by one of her biographers as "tall, thin, energetic, having masculine courage, religious fervor and a motherly nature," was not so easily subdued. Desiring to raise Washington Seminary to the level of Troy, Foster often shocked and dismayed her board of trustees. She did not back down when she found herself at odds with the men who had hired her, but, in her own words, "where we could not agree . . . [we] often agreed to disagree" (Branton 1977, 7). Nevertheless, apparently using both intimidation tactics and "feminine sway," Foster "frequently got her own way" (Alexander 1957, 2). Under her direction, Washington Seminary became one of the best women's schools in its region, offering a level of rigorous instruction similar to Troy in sciences, languages, and liberal arts.

Foster embodied the kind of independent woman such an education would inevitably create. When Massachusetts congressman and former U.S. president John Quincy Adams stopped by Washington Female Seminary during a visit to the town in 1843, Foster broke with convention by publicly speaking in front of a mixed audience and most graciously welcomed him to her school. According to the local newspaper, Adams—who was, after all, the son of Abigail Adams, who in her lifetime had expressed unconventional views about women's rights—"was greatly affected" by Foster's courage, and replied warmly:

> This . . . is the first instance in which a lady has addressed me personally, and I trust that all the ladies present will be able sufficiently to enter into my feelings to know that I am more affected by this honor than by any other I could have received. . . . it has been the perpetual instruction of my life to love and revere the female sex. . . .
>
> I therefore conclude by assuring you, Madam, that your reception of me has affected me, as you perceive, more than I can at all express in words, and that I shall offer my best prayers . . . that this institution especially, and all others of a similar kind, designed to form the female mind to wisdom and virtue, may prosper to the end of time. (*Washington Examiner*, Nov. 25, 1843; qtd. in Branton 1977, 9)

It is no wonder that Sarah Foster was "regarded with awe and affection" by her school community (Branton 1977, 16). After this illustrious beginning to her direction of Washington Seminary, the school was well on its way to becoming a hotbed for new ideas and activities for women.

Elizabeth Russell enrolled in Washington Seminary after being handpicked by Sarah Foster Hanna when their paths crossed at the Wheeling Female Seminary. Elizabeth had been fortunate enough to have a female seminary open in her hometown of Wheeling when she was thirteen, after a group of the town's businessmen had taken an interest in establishing such an institution. As a result, before meeting the principal of Washington Seminary, Elizabeth had already received a relatively good education for a girl of her day (although not at the level of Washington Seminary), and she had begun to teach at Wheeling Female Seminary by her late teens (McCreary 1992, 5).

Elizabeth met Sarah Foster Hanna during the 1855–56 school year. Mrs. Hanna, although she had married a man with five children and was now in her fifties, was as energetic as ever, and had agreed to act as the temporary principal of the Wheeling Seminary in addition to Washington Seminary, which was twenty-six miles away. Spending two days a week at Wheeling that year, Mrs. Hanna—always on the lookout for promising protégées—recognized the potential of nineteen-year-old Elizabeth Russell. The year Mrs. Hanna arrived to work at Wheeling Seminary, Elizabeth's mother died—"the first great grief of my life," she later wrote in her journal—and it seems that Elizabeth became quite attached to this new woman in her life, who represented a whole new set of possibilities. At the end of the school year, in 1856, Elizabeth left home for the first time and followed Mrs. Hanna to Pennsylvania, where she became a boarding student at Washington Female Seminary.

There Elizabeth was introduced to an academic world based on Emma Willard's design—a program of study giving women an educational experience mirroring that of the most privileged men. Like men in elite colleges, Elizabeth studied science, mathematics, Latin, and Greek. She was part of a school community that was like a close-knit family—students in male colleges were called "sons" by their faculty; women in Willard-style seminaries were called "daughters"—which helped to give her an ease and confidence around those who were not her actual kin. She was required, like all graduates of Willard-style seminaries, to take her oral exams during finals week in front of the school, the Board of Trustees (who took a "lively interest" in the development of the school's daughters), and the Board of Visitors, consisting of "gentlemen of the place and vicinity" (Branton 1977, 12). These public examinations, which followed the protocol of men's colleges, were no doubt the most obvious way to prove to the school's supporters that the curriculum was not in vain—that women were indeed capable of fully mastering the unconventional subjects they were studying. Although one graduate remembered these public examinations to be "a fearful ordeal . . . for many a timid and sensitive girl" (*Semi-Centennial Celebration* 1886, 23–24; qtd. in Branton 1977, 5), they no doubt were instrumental in giving Washington Seminary's young women the will and the courage to fully reveal their intellectual prowess in public forums, even to mixed audiences of men and women.

By the time Elizabeth Russell arrived at Washington Female Seminary in 1856, it was taken for granted at the school that students would openly discuss and debate women's proper roles and rights in society. While at the seminary, she was exposed to both traditionalist and progressive gender ideologies. During an 1866 reunion of Washington graduates, for example, women who were staunch supporters of the separate-spheres ideology and women who supported the burgeoning women's rights movement all freely spoke their minds. A representative of the class of 1850, Mrs. Amanda Christy Brown, championed marriage and motherhood as a sign of success for Washington graduates, stating, "I do not know that any of our Class have distinguished themselves as literary characters, but a great many have been successful in winning and holding *one heart,* and thereby have been gradually promoted to the honor of wife, mother and housekeeper. These positions, *efficiently filled,* constitute educated woman's highest sphere" (*Quarter-Centennial Re-Union* 1866, 14).

At the same meeting, a Mrs. C. LeMoyne Wills, representative of the class of 1841, relayed a most powerful speech on human equality to her fellow alumnae, as well as to the Washington Seminary faculty and administration:

> The time will come, and is not very distant. . . . when great and noble careers shall be open to *all* who are fitted to follow them; when the woman, whose duty and necessity requires her to earn her own living, shall not be obliged to choose between the schoolroom, the needle, and the wash-tub; but may be guided by her capabilities and her natural tastes. . . .
>
> When women are prepared to maintain a position of equality, it will be readily acknowledged that they are the *equals* of man, in rights and intellects; and their civil and political influence will be found as beneficial and refining in the State, and in society, as their social and religious influence has proved.
>
> Then, *universal suffrage* will follow universal freedom, no longer restricted by color, or race, or *sex*, and we shall all be alike before the law, as before our God. (*Quarter-Centennial Re-Union* 1866, 9–10)

Having been introduced to such ideas, the young Elizabeth Russell, who was the valedictorian of the class of 1859, likely had her eye toward a life other than that of an efficient housekeeper. She had many years ahead of her, however, before any such youthful hopes for reaching her potential were to be fully realized.

Breakdown and Redemption: Elizabeth Russell and the Methodist Episcopal Church

After graduation, twenty-two-year-old Elizabeth returned home to Virginia, where she worked at odd jobs for a few years. She spent some time as a governess with a family in the Allegheny Mountains, and she was listed in the 1860 Wheeling Census as a photograph painter. The years of the Civil War were chaotic in Wheeling; Elizabeth witnessed the divisiveness of the war firsthand, as Virginians west of the Allegheny Mountains—who had little to do with the slaveholding plantation culture of southeastern Virginia—balked at Virginia's Confederate status and rallied to become an independent state. With the aid of Abraham Lincoln, West Virginia became a state of the Union in 1863, and Wheeling its temporary capital.

That same year, Elizabeth's sister Julia married George Ephraim Chapman, and the couple moved to Cumberland, Maryland, where Ephraim found work as a merchant and studied to be a physician. Julia soon began bearing children, four of whom died in infancy or early childhood, one who became disabled in early childhood after a fall, and three who grew up without mishap (McCreary 1992, 7–8). Not long after Julia's marriage, Elizabeth moved in with her sister and brother-in-law. Propriety would not allow Elizabeth, now in her late twenties, to live alone, and perhaps living with her sister was preferable to living with her father and his new wife, or being a full-time governess; or perhaps her sister asked her to come. In her journal written decades later, Elizabeth merely stated that she "had a call to Cumberland." While there, Elizabeth found employment as a teacher, a position she kept for the next six years.

As part of the Chapman family, Elizabeth found that her life came to be dictated by Ephraim's career direction, as Julia's was. When Ephraim became a railroad company doctor, he was transferred to Piedmont, West Virginia. So the family, including Elizabeth, moved to Piedmont, where Elizabeth again found employment as a teacher.

In 1872, Elizabeth had, in her own words, "a complete nervous breakdown." As she described it years later in her journal, "The physician"—perhaps Ephraim himself—"told me I must stop teaching or I would die. I sold my school equipment to the School Board of the town and never expected to enter the schoolroom again." Now thirty-six years old, Elizabeth was facing the very real possibility of spending her remaining years in infirmity and decay before entering an early grave (she was, after all, only a few years younger than her mother had been when she entered her deathbed). Elizabeth was sent on a retreat to the Glades of Pennsylvania "for the restoration of nerves," but finding no relief from what today would likely be considered a serious case of depression, she returned to the Chapman residence in Piedmont and continued to suffer for many months. Ephraim was then transferred to Keyser, West Virginia, and the family, including Elizabeth, relocated once again.

Elizabeth was saved by Methodism. In 1873, now an "old maid" and a virtual invalid, she attended a Methodist camp meeting in Moundsville, West Virginia, with the encouragement and assistance of a friend. The experience dramatically transformed her life.

Elizabeth had been attached to the Methodist Church since her youth but never experienced full sanctification and holiness until attending the Moundsville camp meeting. Evangelical Methodism expected individuals, even those raised in Christian homes, to go through a process of conversion, when they fully and consciously gave their hearts to Christ; beyond this, many Methodist leaders encouraged converts to open themselves up to the transforming power of sanctification, which would help them lead perfect, holy lives like Christ's. In her journal, Elizabeth identified the date of her conversion as February 11, 1852, when as a fifteen-year-old girl she had attended a local Methodist revival led by a minister skilled at bringing "a great number of young people . . . into the church." At this young age, she wrote, "I heard a voice say 'come unto me.' I came to Jesus and found in Him a satisfying portion." However, despite this experience of youthful religious ecstasy, faith did not become the center of her life until more than twenty years later.

At the Moundsville camp meeting in 1873, Elizabeth experienced what she believed to be a divine healing and was filled with a vigor that would propel her into a new and completely unexpected phase of her life. This particular meeting was a most notable event, as an estimated five thousand individuals "from at least a dozen States of the Union" came to celebrate "a National Love-Feast" (*Wheeling Daily Intelligencer,* Aug. 27, 1873). Many worshipers, including Elizabeth, camped for a number of days in large tents on the grounds. Like most camp meeting grounds, the setting was a beautiful natural environment, charged with the energy of revival. On the day of the keynote sermon, the local newspaper commented that "[a] more beautiful Sunday never smiled on the hills and valleys of West Virginia," perfect for a meeting that "was one of great power, thrilling all hearts with the story of the all-cleansing blood." The preacher leading the camp meeting, the Reverend John S. Inskip, informed those gathered that the focus of the meeting was "holiness, entire sanctification, and perfect love" achieved through purification from one's sins through Jesus' blood.[9]

9. The Reverend John S. Inskip (1816–1884) was a famous Methodist Episcopal preacher and a leader of the holiness movement. As the first president of the National

Following a typical conversion narrative, Elizabeth's journal account of her experience emphasized her initial inability to grasp the message of holiness. "I wandered over the camp grounds that first day and met many old friends whom I had not seen for ten years, but I thought little of the object of that camp meeting," she stated, "then one friend and another began to talk to me about perfect love or sanctification, but I was not interested." A breakthrough came when in the boarding tent Elizabeth "was thrown in close relation to a Mrs. Ladd, a sainted Quaker lady who was helpful to me spiritually." Apparently, numerous individuals from other denominations had attended this camp meeting, helping Methodists spread the message of holiness; in his sermon, Reverend Inskip stated that "they are coming to the rescue from other denominations—all hail! Brethren we welcome you; Presbyterians, Baptists and Quakers! Oh yes, that band of heroes marked by their peculiar dress, Shout the blood!" The night after Elizabeth's spiritual encounter with the Quaker woman, she slept well for the first time in over a year. In her journal account, rainwater baptized her as she was in the depths of a transformative sleep: "It rained hard and the tent leaked above my berth and my pillow and the bed cover were wet but I did not waken until late." When she woke up the next morning she was ready to embrace the minister's call for inner renewal.

The sermons about sanctification at the meeting, Elizabeth wrote, "won me entirely for holiness." Resolving to dedicate her life completely to Christ's path, she "returned home well in soul and body" and believed for the rest of her life that "there was a divine touch in my healing." After her healing, she immediately returned to teaching when the new school year began, stating that she had "never felt better in my life."

She also began to look for new ways to live out her dedication to God through the Methodist Episcopal Church. The newly formed Woman's Foreign Missionary Society of the Methodist Episcopal Church (North), which had been active for four years at the time of Russell's healing, gave

---

Camp Meeting Association for the Promotion of Holiness, he was instrumental in organizing numerous camp meeting events after the Civil War (see McDonald and Searles [1885] 1985).

her the outlet she desired, and she began to volunteer for a local chapter. The WFMS strongly supported the holiness movement within Methodism. Missions historian Dana Robert points out that influential leaders of the organization promoted holiness with the belief that the experience of sanctification "removed one's original sin and made possible a life consecrated to God's work in the world" (Robert 1996, 146). The pages of *The Heathen Woman's Friend* emphasized "the inseparability of 'entire consecration and personal devotion to Christ, and love for the perishing'" (WFMS, *HWF,* 1881, 13, no. 4:93; qtd. in Robert 1996, 147).

Elizabeth quickly moved into a leadership position within the WFMS, and while continuing to teach in Keyser, she took on the secretaryship of the West Virginia branch of the WFMS. After six years of organizing and leading WFMS activity in West Virginia, at the age of forty-two, she was ready to give herself completely to the work; as recorded in her journal, "I answered the mission call to the foreign field. I offered my life in service to the W.F.M.S." Seven years after a nervous breakdown, during which she was told to expect nothing but a future of idleness and decay, Elizabeth had found the most important work of her life: a forty-year missionary career in Japan. She expressed her experience of divine intervention in an Easter essay she wrote for *The Heathen Woman's Friend,* in which she exulted, "A sinless Saviour has invaded our world. . . . Dwelling upon this new glory, this beauty of holiness, soul after soul has been translated from darkness to light, has been Christ-likened, changed from glory unto glory, until even the inspired cry out in wondering ecstasy and awe, 'It doth not yet appear what we shall be'" (Russell 1876, 228).

3

"Who Are We That We Should Fight Against the Holy Spirit?"

The Rise of the American Women's Mission Movement

> On the evening of November 2, [1869,] Bedford St. Church, New York, was crowded to the doors with a sympathetic audience to see this strange sight, two single ladies about to sail the ocean to a new and untried task, with no pledge of support save that of a handful of women!
>
> . . . The sailing of these women aroused the women of the Church as nothing else could have done.
>
> —Mary Isham, *Valorous Ventures*, 1936

> If the Holy Spirit did not bless the public work of women, if He did not use them in public speaking, their failure would be apparent to all. . . . But if, as is unquestionably the fact, the Holy Spirit does use our sisters and blesses their labors in the conversion and edification of souls, who are we that we should fight against the Holy Spirit . . . ?
>
> —Reverend James W. Bashford
> *The Bible and Woman*, ca. 1888

Elizabeth Russell's experience of sanctification, holiness, and healing coincided with the dawn of the women's mission movement. After the Civil War, missionary fever had swept through America's Protestant denominations, bringing Protestant women's enthusiasm for missions to new heights for decades to come. Nearly forty denominational women's foreign mission societies were formed in North America between 1868 and 1900 (Montgomery 1910, appendix). Women's participation in foreign missions skyrocketed, and by 1915 there were more than three million women on the membership rosters of female missionary societies (Hill 1985, 3). Periodicals such as the Methodist Episcopal Church's *The Heathen Woman's Friend,* Congregationalists' *Life and Light for Heathen Women,* and the Presbyterian Church's *Woman's Work for Woman and Our Mission Field* launched the women's missionary movement by convincing tens of thousands of American women to sacrifice, either financially or through their own labor as missionaries, to spread Christianity throughout the world.

An avid supporter of women's foreign missions from the time of her camp meeting healing in 1873, Elizabeth Russell was heavily influenced by the rhetoric of the movement. Like many women who supported missions, Russell was particularly moved by stories and images of the women in India, which dominated the pages of *The Heathen Woman's Friend* and other early publications of women's missionary societies. In 1876, while serving as secretary of the West Virginia branch of the WFMS of the Methodist Episcopal Church, Russell wrote an article for *The Heathen Woman's Friend* in which she repeated the much-circulated rhetoric about the coming triumph of Christianity over the bondage of Indian women in zenanas (secluded quarters for high-caste women), stating,

> To-day, Brahma and Buddha sit pale and trembling on their thrones, as Messiah is winning the homage of Earth's millions. The reports of our missionaries show a growing appreciation on the part of heathen women themselves. They tell of aching hearts in zenana prisons, longing for help and for light. . . . Let us not faint nor grow weary, but haste to tell them of Him who, by His glorious resurrection, hath brought life and immortality to light. (Russell 1876, 228)

When she applied for a missionary position six years after her healing (thereby escaping what she perhaps considered her own prison), Russell requested an appointment to India, where Isabella Thoburn, the first missionary sponsored by the WFMS, had been laboring for nearly ten years. The WFMS indicated that her wish would be granted, and she was scheduled to sail in October 1879. During the summer of 1879, however, a General Board missionary in Japan, the Rev. John C. Davison, wrote a letter to the WFMS pleading for experienced women teachers to be sent to Nagasaki. As a result, two weeks before Russell was planning to sail for India, she received word that her assignment had been changed to Japan. She wrote in her journal, "I was somewhat disappointed for I had always had my heart set on India." Another WFMS missionary who also had been assigned to India, Jennie Gheer ("whom I had never seen or heard of," wrote Russell), was reappointed to join Russell in starting WFMS work in Nagasaki. Russell met Gheer in "Frisco," as Russell wrote in her journal, where they "sailed on the 'Gaelic,' a steamer of 3000 tons, on October 25th." This trip was the first time Russell had ever seen San Francisco, the Pacific Ocean, or a steamer ship. It was the first time she had ever been out of the United States. Elizabeth Russell had embarked on a new life in an unknown land, as a professional missionary for the Woman's Foreign Missionary Society of the Methodist Episcopal Church.

By the time Elizabeth Russell was appointed as a missionary in 1879, the WFMS of the Methodist Episcopal Church, founded ten years earlier, had grown into the largest missionary society operated independently by Protestant women. Its work was already becoming legendary, as its publications featured the adventures and successes of missionary women for an ever-expanding readership. Hagiographic in style, WFMS portrayals of foreign missionaries indicated that these women had chosen a noble alternative to the traditional paths available to women in the United States.

Circulating for years in various Methodist Episcopal publications, highly stylized descriptions of the origins of the WFMS suggested the presence of God's hand in every detail of the society's development. According to one story, Isabella Thoburn received her calling when her missionary brother was inspired by a vulture to write his unmarried sister to encourage her to join him in India. As James Thoburn was pondering how to reach Indian women, the large bird, "wheeling overhead, dropped a feather from its wing," and he was moved to use it as a pen to write the historic letter, having received his inspiration from "above" (Isham 1936, 11). When a small group of Methodist Episcopal women met in Boston in 1869 to organize the missionary society that would send Isabella to India, they braved the harsh elements, traveling to the meeting through "the most famous rainy day since the flood" in order to get their work done (13). There was much heralding of the courage of "[w]omen who had been called out from the quiet seclusion of their homes to do this untried work" (Baker [1896] 1987, 30). Month after month, *The Heathen Woman's Friend* sent out a rallying cry to all the women of the Methodist Episcopal Church; one issue triumphantly proclaimed, "We are seven hundred thousand. This mighty host, redeemed by the precious blood of Christ, should do something for the greater host of heathen women for whom Christ died, but who have not heard of his name. The army has been organized. Banners are floating in the air. Hard battles have been fought, and won. But there is much land to be possessed. We need an army of occupation, as well as an aggressive force. So we call for recruits. We want all the women of the church to engage in this holy war" (WFMS, *HWF* 1874, 5, no. 7:588).

Literature written by supporters of women's missions indicated that the work of the WFMS should strike readers with awe and reverence, especially for the women who had given up what were assumed to be happy lives in the United States to brave the wilds of "heathen lands." Isabella Thoburn, for example, achieved a saintlike status during her lifetime and beyond, something very few unmarried Protestant women could expect in the United States. When she embarked on her first trip to India in 1869, along with fellow WFMS missionary Dr. Clara Swain, enraptured crowds came to their send-off at Bedford Street Church in New York, and fans frequently asked the editors of *The Heathen Woman's Friend* to print more news about the society's first missionary. After her death in India in 1901—having lived and worked there for more than thirty years—Thoburn was portrayed by a biographer as the wise counselor of "Christians, Hindus, Mohammedans, the rich, the poor," all of whom sought her advice (Oldham 1902, 30). She had, in the words of her brother, "a knowledge of the great forces, mental, moral, and political, which were affecting the world in which she lived," something she was able to put to great use in the mission field (Thoburn 1903, 19).

Elizabeth Russell, following the footsteps of Isabella Thoburn, did have strong religious sensibilities motivating her to become a missionary—she was convinced that sanctification and holiness had dramatically transformed her life and could transform the lives of others—but, like other women who became missionaries in this period, she was also drawn to foreign missions because she had few other career paths as attractive as this one. Although the path of the missionary was not an easy one, by joining this exciting new movement, Russell was freed from the constraints of her family, her community, and American culture as a whole. She was sent into a world where, as a white American woman, she would have opportunities not available at home, while at the same time she would be lauded as a selfless servant by the community she left behind.

Methodism, Domesticity, and Women's Holy Calling

The spiritual journey that eventually brought Elizabeth Russell into the mission movement reflects the larger evangelical experience of nineteenth-century Protestant women; her breakdown and redemption reveal the constraints and possibilities women encountered in the religious and cultural landscape of the era. As Nancy A. Hardesty states in *Women Called to Witness,* the "twisted strand of women's history in the nineteenth century" included radical evangelical revivalism that emboldened women for public action, as well as notions of gender and biblical literalism that emphasized women's "special nature" and "separate sphere of usefulness" (1999, 2). It was through this ideological mix that Protestant women sought paths to improve their lives and the lives of others.[1]

By the time the WFMS was formed in 1869, Methodism had evolved from its origins as a radical offshoot of the Church of England to become the largest form of Protestantism in the United States. As such, it was embracing and influencing mainstream gender ideologies, while at the same time continuing earlier theologies and practices that challenged nineteenth-century gender divisions. In the early days of the republic, Methodism

1. Because women were politicized by encountering numerous barriers to fulfilling their holy callings, one can trace a direct sequence of events, in the words of Hardesty, from "women's earliest organizations to promote missions and charity in the early 1800s . . . to the passage of the Nineteenth Amendment in 1920" (1999, xii).

played an important role in shifting popular consciousness away from an earlier Christian emphasis on women's sinfulness and enlightenment-era disdain for feminine emotion. During the Second Great Awakening and the continuing nineteenth-century holiness movement, evangelical Methodism helped to popularize the emotional experience of the divine, establishing "heart-felt" spirituality as a legitimate, even preferred, mode of religious expression. As emotion was often associated with the feminine, women came to be seen as naturally religious, and they enjoyed relative public freedom in early Methodist circles, including public speaking, if they felt called by God (Duvall 1928, 65). Drawing on the Methodist belief in sanctification by the Holy Spirit, Methodist women throughout the nineteenth century claimed their religious authority came directly from God rather than any earthly authority. Such claims could empower women, at times, to step outside traditionally prescribed women's roles.

However, as the nineteenth century progressed, American Methodism began to shift, in the words of John Higham (1969), from "boundlessness to consolidation." Methodists, who had traditionally rejected an educational requirement for religious leadership, began to codify Methodist experience, social goals, and theology, and began to found colleges and seminaries for the purpose of training denominational leaders (Schneider 1993, 149).[2] As Methodists began to move into mainstream, middle-class respectability and religious professionalism during this period of consolidation, the ideology of domesticity became firmly entrenched in Methodist discourses about gender. Even though nineteenth-century Methodism was an important influence in developing the ideals of feminine morality and spirituality, as Methodists became more "respectable," they sought to domesticate women's religious impulses. Methodists melded the prevailing ideology of domesticity with their own theological views, however.

The appropriation of the domestic ideal, for Methodists, was part of a move to keep religion unpolluted by the world, and women were called upon to create a haven for Methodist ideals in the domestic sphere. As A.

2. Although Methodists founded some schools from their earliest days in the United States, Methodist education really took off between 1835 and 1860, when more than two hundred schools and colleges were founded (see Duvall 1928, 65).

Gregory Schneider points out, while early American Methodism was in many ways a product of the looser social order and democratic freedom of the new republic, as the denomination became more defined and institutionalized, "Methodist reflections on the roles of the religious community and the Christian home in the republic promoted these agencies as the needed centripetal counterbalance to the centrifugal forces of American liberty" (Schneider 1993, 150). As Methodists identified sacred space with "the church, with home, and with women as the 'natural' symbol of religion and domesticity," Methodists came to believe, like other nineteenth-century Americans, that the purpose of the home (and homebound women) was to protect the purity of religion from the larger society so that, in turn, unsullied religion could uplift that society. Thus, in writing about the domestic sphere, one Methodist writer stated that "[o]ur home is a sanctuary too sacred to be invaded" (*Western Christian Advocate,* Jan. 25, 1837, 72; qtd. in Schneider 1993, 157), revealing the growing Methodist movement to keep the world out of the sacred space of the home, and to keep women, as the protectors of this space, out of the world.

As Methodists sacralized the home, they also "sacralized Woman, the center of the home" (Schneider 1993, 170). Thus, despite the limitations placed on women in this scheme, the continuing value placed on their spirituality was an ever-present loophole in the ideology of domesticity. Building on notions of women's sacred responsibilities to protect and uplift family and society, Methodist women continued to claim the leadership of the Holy Spirit to legitimate their religious activities beyond the domestic sphere.

Although Methodism had professionalized its clergy by midcentury, camp meetings and revivals continued to be a central component of the Methodist experience, which provided settings where women received radical calls from God. Like Elizabeth Russell found in the 1870s, women had ample opportunity to find religious inspiration outside of the confines of a carefully conducted parish. Even as Methodism became a respectable, middle-class religious institution, it gave rise to some of the most prominent women involved in nineteenth-century religious and political activism, such as Phoebe Palmer, Frances Willard, and the Rev. Dr. Anna Howard Shaw.

Many Methodists were influenced by the leadership of Phoebe Palmer, a holiness revivalist, who argued that "for women, as well as men, response to God's call in public witness was not a matter of preference but a necessity." Palmer asserted that, in order to convert as many people as possible, "it was critical that the church neither neglect nor repress the gifts of the Spirit, even or especially when they [were] bestowed on women" (Lindley 1996, 120). She influenced other prominent Methodist women to actively support women's religious leadership. For example, the famous leader of the Women's Christian Temperance Union, Frances Willard, became an outspoken advocate of women's ordination in the Methodist Episcopal Church after committing herself to a life of holiness at a revival led by Palmer (Schmidt 1993, 237). Willard directly confronted the Methodist Episcopal Church on this issue when she published *Woman in the Pulpit* (1888), in which she contended that women's ordination had a biblical basis. However, while a number of women applied to the Methodist Episcopal Church for ordination in the late nineteenth century, even with recommendations from their regional conferences, the MEC General Conference rejected women's ordination until the 1950s.

In the 1870s—the same decade that Elizabeth Russell became involved in the WFMS—Anna Howard Shaw had petitioned unsuccessfully for ordination within the Methodist Episcopal Church. Finding that branch of Methodism too embroiled in controversy over women's leadership roles, Shaw finally became an ordained minister with the Methodist Protestant Church in 1880. Politicized by the hopes and the disappointments they experienced in the church, Willard and Shaw eventually became nationally recognized voices within the woman's suffrage movement; Shaw even succeeded Susan B. Anthony as president of the National American Woman Suffrage Association in 1904. While Willard and Shaw were exceptional in that they were superstars among prosuffrage Americans (and villains in the minds of the antisuffragists), they represented a growing number of Methodists who came to support women's ecclesiastical and political rights by the end of the nineteenth century. Women's leadership increasingly became a topic of debate within Methodist circles as the century drew to a close. Although women involved in missions initially sidestepped this debate, they ultimately became a major force in liberalizing Methodists' perspectives on the issue.

Origins of Protestant Women's Missions

Denied ecclesiastical equality in most denominations, numerous late-nineteenth-century Protestant women focused their energies on developing a large-scale women's mission movement. This movement was not only girded by religious and gender ideologies emphasizing women's natural propensity for such work, but it was also rooted in a strong American evangelical heritage of postmillennialist faith, which had driven American Protestant movements since the antebellum era (see Ginzberg 2000; Moorhead 1999); the idea of bringing God's kingdom on earth through missions had occupied Protestant women from the earliest days of the republic. Women called to missions met less resistance than women called to the ordained ministry. A zealous, self-sacrificing, and even (as some might conclude) masochistic missionary spirit was deeply embedded in American Protestantism, which stood in tension with the domestic ideal of protecting women in the private sphere. These ideals of religion and gender were utilized in multiple, often conflicting discourses about women in missions over the course of the nineteenth century.

Mission-minded women throughout American Protestantism had long admired Ann Hasseltine Judson (1789–1826), who, in 1812, was one of the first women to leave her home in the United States for a life overseas as a missionary wife. She is a compelling example of a Protestant icon who stood in tension with competing ideals of the genteel wife and mother. For many, Ann Judson was a model of womanly courage and religious fervor because she left domestic comforts behind—risking everything to follow her calling. Shortly before her twenty-second birthday, according to an 1831 biography, Ann felt "an ardent desire to be instrumental of spreading the knowledge of the Redeemer's name in a heathen land." Even though no other American woman had ever gone overseas to become involved in missionary work, and many of Ann's peers dismissed the thought of a white woman living in a "heathen land" as a "wild, romantic undertaking," Ann was convinced that God wanted her to reject the gendered expectations of her society for a higher cause. She wrote in her journal, "I would rather go to India, among the heathen, notwithstanding the almost insurmountable difficulties in the way, than to stay at home" (qtd. in Knowles [1831] 1987, 46, 48).

For those who ventured out to unknown lands as missionaries in this era, the likelihood of sacrificing life and limb for their work was much higher than for those who journeyed to established missions at the end of the nineteenth century. When Congregationalist missionary Adoniram Judson asked Ann's father for her hand in marriage, he did not paint a pretty picture of the life ahead of them in foreign lands. Presenting his marriage proposal to Mr. Hasseltine, Adoniram stated,

> I have now to ask, whether you can consent to part with your daughter early next spring, to see her no more in this world; whether you can consent to her departure for a heathen land, and her subjection to the hardships and sufferings of a missionary life; whether you can consent to her exposure to the dangers of the ocean; to the fatal influence of the Southern climate of India; to every kind of want and distress; to degradation, insult, persecution, and perhaps a violent death. (Knowles [1831] 1987, 49)

These are not words to warm the heart of a father toward a prospective son-in-law. Adoniram could only promise that through consenting, Mr. Hasseltine would have "hope of soon meeting your daughter in the world of glory [i.e., heaven], with a crown of righteousness." Ann and Adoniram married two weeks before they sailed from Salem, Massachusetts, to Calcutta, under the auspices of the Congregationalist Church's missionary organization, the American Board of Commissioners for Foreign Missions. (During their journey, however, the Judsons decided to become Baptists and thus after 1814 were supported by the Baptist General Commission for Foreign Missions [Robert 1996, 43–46].) During the long voyage across the sea, Ann prepared for her work mentally by avidly studying scripture and physically by jumping rope (Harvey 1911, 42).

After their arrival and subsequent relocation to Burma, the Judsons suffered greatly like most early missionaries, yet they doggedly pursued their work. Over the years, their child contracted smallpox and Adoniram was jailed when war broke out between Burma and Britain. Spending nearly fourteen years in Burma before dying in her thirties, Ann worked tirelessly with her husband in translating scripture into Burmese, and she also became proficient enough in Siamese (Thai) that she was the first to translate Christian scripture—the Gospel of Matthew—into that language, in addition to writing an English-language history of the Burmese mission. Later hailed as "one of the most remarkable women of her age," she was valorized for her sacrificial dedication to missions and complete acculturation to a non-Western society. "So thoroughly did she identify herself with Burma," wrote a Methodist admirer in 1912, "that when she died there of fever, in 1826, her last exclamation was in the Burmese language" (Harvey 1911, 42). An icon such as Ann Judson represented the long-standing potential of Protestant fervor to open up unconventional possibilities for women.

Woman's Work for Woman

Although many missionaries spent years, often decades, away from the United States—an experience that led many to be more attached to their new host society than to the land of their birth—the enterprise in which they were involved was heavily influenced by imperialist assumptions regarding the West's superiority, including ideas about the superiority of women's status in Western civilization. American Protestants imagined that the United States most closely reflected God's kingdom on earth, and that their country should therefore serve as a model for all the world. When U.S. Methodists organized their first denominational foreign mission board in 1819 (often called the General Board or the Parent Board), Methodist women quickly established auxiliaries to support the cause, citing their desire to share the privileges they associated with Christian civilization with women around the world. Although Methodist women had limited success in pursuing mission work for women until the independent Woman's Foreign Missionary Society was established explicitly for this purpose fifty years later (Robert 1996, 127), their interest in this endeavor was present from the earliest days of Methodist missions, as American women also embraced the country's "manifest destiny." When the organizers of the first auxiliary circulated a bulletin in 1819 to publicize their organization to Methodist women, they stated, "Shall we, who dwell in ease and plenty, whose tables are loaded with the bounties of Providence, and whose persons are clothed with the fine-wrought materials of the Eastern looms . . . deny the small subscription this institution solicits to carry the glad tidings of free salvation to the scattered inhabitants of the wilderness?" (qtd. in Baker [1896] 1987, 9). This rhetoric—contrasting the luxury and freedom experienced by women in Protestant America with the women in the wilderness—continued throughout the nineteenth century and was a driving logic behind the organization of the WFMS.

In 1867, after a number of individuals within Protestant denominations began expressing interest in expanding "woman's work for woman" in missions, Methodist Episcopal missionaries William and Clementina Butler became two of the most important early champions of the establishment of independent women's missionary societies. Setting the tone for the women's mission movement, the Butlers publicized their belief that the absence of Christianity in India was the cause of a grotesque degradation of the female sex. In their view, the first two orphan girls they sheltered could be seen as symbols of "helpless Indian womanhood"—one was "a dirty little waif, half starved, pockmarked, [and] blind in one eye," and the other had been rescued by English soldiers after having been "buried alive, with only her face exposed as she waited death" (Isham 1936, 10).[3] Such sensationalist descriptions of female oppression outside of Protestant cultures would dominate the early rhetoric of American women's missions, adding urgency to their call for Christian women to take the lead in saving the world's female population.

The Butlers and like-minded missionaries worked to convince men on various denominational mission boards to support a bold new foreign missions strategy: developing woman-run missionary organizations for the purpose of recruiting unmarried women to engage directly in professional missionary work. They stressed that "missionary wives in the field were overwhelmed by family responsibilities, but that single women could give

3. The Indian girl's rescue by British soldiers was likely charged with symbolic significance for the Butlers as well, since missionaries of this era generally supported British colonial endeavors.

themselves completely to the needs of indigenous women" (Robert 1996, 128). Images of the missionary husband and wife working side by side for the same cause—such as the Judsons—were downplayed by promoters of this new mission strategy.

Like the leaders of any movement that successfully opened new paths for women in the nineteenth century, the Butlers emphasized that men and women would continue to have separate spheres of usefulness, even as women took on professional roles. The Butlers and others who supported creating independent women's foreign missionary societies reasoned that since many cultures around the world had rigid gender divisions, missionary women's work was vital for reaching half of the world's population, since only women could have access to other women. The Butlers, emphasizing that "little progress could be made" in the salvation of India "until the women were reached," stated that male missionaries "faced a shut door and the key was not in their hands. Only women could enter there. . . . to reach the women who fled from the missionary himself" (Isham 1936, 12, 11).[4] Later, the first issue of *The Heathen Woman's Friend* would stress this point, stating optimistically,

> A missionary may preach to crowds of heathen in the market-places, and at the religious fairs, but no woman will be found in his congregation. . . . A Christian woman, however, can go to those villages where the low caste people reside, and can collect in a quiet place a small company of attentive women; she can also go to the private apartments of the women of the higher classes who are kept in seclusion, and be welcomed there; she can open girls' schools among all classes, adapting them to the circumstances of the people, and thus teach Jesus to the women and girls of every caste. (WFMS, *HWF*, 1869, 1, no. 2:10)[5]

4. Note that even though William Butler was promoting women's missions here, his language indicates that the term "missionary" was applied almost exclusively to men at this point, and not to women (even those who were wives of missionaries).

5. The author of this article is referring to India in particular here, the first country to which the WFMS sent missionaries.

Just as men and women in the United States had separate spheres of influence (the public and domestic spheres), so would they have separate spheres of influence in the mission field, according to the logic of these early advocates of women's missions. The separate spheres were now re-drawn, however, so that the missionary woman would have influence in the "woman's sphere" as an independent, unmarried professional, employed by her denomination.

Struggles over Women's Roles

While enjoying some strong support for their cause, the WFMS had to struggle in its early days to earn the respect and trust of prominent men in the Methodist Episcopal Church. The idea of an organization run and operated entirely by women for the purpose of sending unmarried female missionaries to foreign lands "excited genuine alarm"—as James Thoburn sardonically stated years later (WFMS, *WMF,* 1906, 38, no. 9:319)—despite the accommodating rhetoric of the movement's supporters. Individual men in Protestant denominations were loath to give women the reins to develop their own mission societies. The initial goal of those who promoted women's missions was to form an interdenominational women's foreign mission society, but this initiative was rebuffed by most church officials, who were concerned that this would divert attention and financial contributions away from their own denominational mission boards. The Butlers and their supporters then began to work on developing women's missionary societies within individual denominations, but their suggestion that women take on a leadership role in missions at the same level as their fellow churchmen met much resistance. Some encouraging headway was made in 1868, however, when Ned Clark, the secretary of the Congregationalist American Board, supported the women of his denomination in forming the first women's foreign missionary society, officially named the Woman's Board of Missions (Robert 1996, 128).

In 1869, Mrs. Butler helped Methodist Episcopal women take matters into their own hands, and a small group of women organized the second women's foreign missionary society in the United States, the Woman's

Foreign Missionary Society of the Methodist Episcopal Church.[6] During their first meetings, a number of bishops' wives agreed to serve as officers of the organization (Baker [1896] 1987, 22). When word that the women had created an autonomous missionary society reached men in charge of the general mission society of the Methodist Episcopal Church (the General Board), a flurry of debate ensued, and in the following weeks "much was written and said" over the women's unorthodox actions (Isham 1936, 16).

Two of the secretaries of the General Board, the Rev. Dr. John Price Durbin and Rev. Dr. William L. Harris, traveled from New York to Boston, where the WFMS had been organized, to convince the women to give up the project. Like leaders of other general missionary boards, Durbin and Harris resisted the formation of an independent woman's missionary society, with most of their stated opposition "couched in terms of the danger of fragmenting fund-raising efforts for missions" (Hill 1985, 49). Although they stated that they "found the missionary spirit manifested by the ladies worthy of all commendation," they made clear their "fear that their success would interfere with the receipts of the Parent Board" (Isham 1936, 16). Somewhat contradictorily, Durbin also charged that the women were incapable of the task they had undertaken; he chided, "Could you ladies make the necessary arrangements for Miss A. to go to India, obtain bills of exchange, take care of her on the voyage, provide a home when she arrives at her destination, and so forth? No, your work is to forward the money for Miss A. to [the General Board headquarters in] New York." Despite Durbin's desire for them to take an auxiliary status to his board, the organizers of the WFMS stood their ground, stating, "We women feel that we have organized an independent Society. We will be as dutiful children

6. After the Congregationalist and Methodist Episcopal women's foreign missionary societies were formed, other early denominational women's foreign missionary societies included the Woman's Foreign Missionary Society of the Presbyterian Church (North) (1870); the Woman's Baptist Foreign Missionary Society (1873); the Woman's Parent Mite Missionary Society of the African Methodist Episcopal Church (1874); and the Woman's Board of Foreign Missions of the Reformed Church in America (1875). See the appendix in Montgomery (1910) for an extensive listing of women's foreign mission societies formed in the nineteenth century.

to the Church authorities, but through our own organization we may do a work which no other can accomplish" (Butler 1929, 110).

The desire of the WFMS organizers to develop a standard practice of encouraging unmarried women to become missionaries was also part of the reason for the General Board's concern. The General Board had resisted sending unmarried women to the mission field (including Isabella Thoburn), and, although Durbin had accomplished a great feat in building up Methodist missions (see Richey 2003), he was later criticized for failing to fully harness the energies of Methodist women for missionary work. William F. Oldham, in his 1902 biography of Isabella Thoburn, stated:

> Dr. Durbin, one of the strong men of the Church and the secretary of the society, wails: "If I wanted fifty young ladies, I could find them in a week; but when I want five young men, I must search for them a year or more." That it might be possible that God was moving the hearts of the young women, and that they might be exceedingly serviceable in the evangelization of the darkened peoples of the earth, seems not to have entered the male mind. (15–16)

When the secretaries of the General Board realized that the women were determined to be independent of the church's male-controlled mission society, and that these women were supported by some leading men of the church (most of the women in question, after all, were the wives of respected missionaries and bishops), a compromise was reached. The compromise had elements that seem to have been designed to hamper the growth of the WFMS. In order to receive the approval of the General Board, WFMS leaders were compelled to make significant concessions, such as agreeing to severely limit their fund-raising strategies. The WFMS constitution had the stamp of Dr. Durbin's qualifications throughout, as it stated:

> [T]his Society, though not auxiliary to the General Missionary Society, should work in harmony with it, seeking its counsel and approval in all its work. . . .
>
> No public collections should be taken, but an effort should be made to interest every lady of each congregation, where such a society is organized, to do something especially for heathen women, in addition to

> what she may already be doing for the general missionary cause. (WFMS, *HWF,* 1869, 1, no. 1:3–4)

Since the WFMS accepted that they were not to solicit funds at public gatherings (such as church meetings), *The Heathen Woman's Friend* became their primary means for raising money to support women's missions. Articles in the *Friend* urged women to give beyond what they would normally contribute to the missionary cause in order to support women in missions, stating that it should "be clearly understood that on no account ought the regular Church missionary contributions to be lessened. Not one dollar should be taken from those" (WFMS, *HWF,* 1869, 1, no. 1:2).

The first issue of the magazine also had an article by Durbin himself, which suggested that unmarried women should view the missionary path as a solemn sacrifice of their natural place in the domestic sphere, rather than as an entirely positive choice. He stated that women who "may have been weaned from worldly ambitions and desires by some untoward events or grievous afflictions" might validly be accepted in the mission field, but he warned that "no woman should aspire to serve in Christian missions . . . who cannot regard such service as a sacrifice unto God, a whole burnt-offering of body, soul, and spirit" (WFMS, *HWF,* 1869, 1, no. 1:7). Like many men of the general mission boards, he could accept the idea of unmarried missionary women only if it was clear that this path was not the ideal for women, and that only women who viewed this path as a sort of martyrdom should be accepted, rather than women who would freely choose the unmarried missionary life over domesticity and motherhood.

Given such resistance to its goals, it is remarkable that the WFMS attained the financial and institutional success that it did. Even though the General Board had put strict limits on the marketing strategies of the WFMS in order to protect its own revenues, Methodist Episcopal women committed to missions still managed to raise funds successfully through the narrow sphere of agency they had as nineteenth-century middle-class women. Calling their fellow churchwomen to sustain their organization through "self-denial and sacrifice" (WFMS, *HWF,* 1869, 1, no. 1:4), they were able to rally tens of thousands of Methodist Episcopal women to find ways of diverting the funds at their disposal—intended for household and personal expenses—to the missionary cause. Methodist women did this by rejecting, to some degree, the prescripts of Victorian consumerism expected of housewives, denying themselves and their households some of the niceties the middle class had come to expect. When Isabella Thoburn offered herself in service to the Woman's Foreign Missionary Society, the organization wasn't quite ready with the funds to support her; however, when the group congregated to discuss this dilemma, one WFMS official "sprang to her feet, saying, 'Shall we lose Miss Thoburn because we have not the needed money in our hands to send her? No! Rather let us walk the streets of Boston in calico dresses, if need be, and save the expense of more costly apparel!'" (Isham 1936, 18).

Eventually, the WFMS became one of the most successful missionary societies of its day, male or female, despite having more fund-raising handicaps than any male-controlled society. At numerous points throughout their publications, the women of the WFMS could hardly refrain from indulging in a bit of gloating. *The Heathen Woman's Friend* announced that after only two years since the 1869 inception of the WFMS, the group's popularity was spreading much more rapidly than the church's male-controlled missionary society. With apparent glee, the author of an 1871 article titled "What Hath God Wrought?" stated, "When the Parent Society was fifteen years old, its receipts were only $18,000 a year. So greatly has God prospered the Church, that its 'gleaners' bring to the garner $20,000 this second year of their work. 12,000 copies of our paper go into the homes of the people. We number our auxiliaries by hundreds, our members by thousands" (WFMS, *HWF,* 1871, 2, no. 7:79). The budget, membership, and overseas projects of the WFMS would continue to grow rapidly in the years to come.

Rhetorical Strategies of the Women's Mission Movement

The Woman's Foreign Missionary Society was able to gain support for women's leadership in missions by effectively integrating into their rhetoric a Methodist theology that validated women's spirituality with Victorian domestic ideology and imperialist discourses. Supporters of the WFMS initially supported their cause by proclaiming that Christian women had a calling from God to sacralize the domestic sphere of heathen lands by becoming professional missionaries themselves.

In 1869, the first issue of *The Heathen Woman's Friend* revealed the initial rhetoric the WFMS used to win support for women's missions: "God's voice is speaking to us—for who can so well do this work as we?" The article continued,

> We well know how close is the relation of the mother to the child, and how important it is that the mother's heart be filled with the love and grace of God if her child is to grow up under Divine influence. . . . We know too how inestimable is the value, and how incalculable the influence of a pure Christian home; and if the influences of such homes are so indispensable in a Christian land, what must be their importance among a people, the depth of whose degradation is, as we are often assured, altogether beyond our realization? (1, no. 1:1)

Illuminated here are three tropes that Methodist women interwove into the ideological foundation of their mission movement. First, their movement was steeped in the Methodist holiness tradition in which all believers, regardless of gender, could receive a divine calling from God. WFMS rhetoric stressed that Methodist women had received their authority directly from God's voice to develop a women's mission society.

Second, as in all Protestant women's missionary societies, the nineteenth-century domestic ideal was heavily utilized to support women's mission work. Reiterating a widely shared assumption among Protestants that a pure and sacred home was necessary to forge strong Christians—and that women were the core of the home—WFMS rhetoric highlighted the importance of Christian women in helping to build Christian homes in non-Christian lands. Also drawing on the domestic ideology of the day that idealized mothers as the bedrock of civilization, supporters of women's missions repeatedly stated that the most important aspect of civilizing non-Western countries was the conversion of heathen women. As an article in the fourth annual report of a Congregationalist women's missionary magazine asserted, "The degradation and oppression of woman is the stronghold of heathenism; and when the lever of the gospel has raised HER, then the whole structure of superstition and idolatry falls" (WBM, *Life and Light for Heathen Women,* 1872, 8–9). In a similar vein, *Woman's Work for Woman,* the magazine of the Woman's Foreign Missionary Society of the Presbyterian Church, stated that women's missionary work had a unique strength in "that it touches society at all of its most sensitive points. It concerns the sacredness of womanhood and motherhood. It molds the plastic character of the young. It exalts and sanctifies the home" (WFMSPC, *WWW,* Jan. 1886, 6). Summing up the motivating logic of the women's mission movement, one missionary simply stated, "You cannot evangelize a country until you convert the women" (WFMS, *HWF* 1869, 1, no. 2:11). By embracing Victorian sentiments regarding the importance of motherhood and domesticity, Protestant women's missions opened up a space of legitimacy for American women who actually did not fulfill domestic roles, as they were able to justify leaving their own domestic sphere to build a vast mission movement focused on employing unmarried missionary women.

Finally, the movement was undergirded by a familiar imperialist discourse—that non-Western lands were in need of the West's redemptive civilization. Like the missionary literature produced by earlier generations, the publications of women's foreign missionary societies detailed the degradation of the natives in non-Christian lands in order to highlight the importance of uplifting these people through mission work. Similar to the way British imperialism was linked to a growing feminist consciousness among British women, as Antoinette M. Burton points out in "The White Woman's Burden" (1990), women in the American context bolstered their confidence to step outside of traditional women's roles when they embraced imperialist discourses to highlight the importance of Western women in civilizing heathen lands. "Let us say to ourselves daily," a contributor to *The Heathen Woman's Friend* charged, "we are jointly and equally responsible with our brothers for the salvation of the world" (WFMS, *HWF,* 1870, 2, no. 5:56). Linking religious conversion with the transformation of societies into Western-style civilizations, at least in the early days of the movement, Protestant women involved in missions were able to move from passive observers to active participants in the work of imperialist nation-building. Another article in *The Heathen Woman's Friend* proclaimed:

> In India there are 193,340,000 inhabitants; in the Chinese Empire, 477,500,00, to say nothing of the multitudes of Turkey, Arabia, and Central Asia. The most of these know nothing of the truths of government, of literature, of medicine, or of religion. . . . It is estimated that there are 300,000,000 of women still in heathen darkness. . . . In life they are shut out from all that makes life desirable to you,—mother, and wife, and daughter. This is what creates a demand,—a demand for educated, devoted, zealous women. (WFMS, *HWF,* 1871, 2, no. 10:139)

By declaring themselves responsible for their benighted "heathen sisters," Western women were embracing an identity of global rescuers and caretakers, which significantly undermined a separate spheres ideology promoting women's submissiveness and seclusion in the private sphere. Even as their mission movement celebrated the ideology of domesticity, evangelical women insisted on creating independent mission societies operated entirely by women, and they encouraged the women of their denominations to leave behind the traditional roles of daughter, wife, and mother in order to become professional missionaries.

Missions as the New Abolition Movement

Finally, the success of the women's mission movement cannot be fully understood without an examination of the Civil War's impact, as it was a catalyst for Protestant women's fervent work to develop missionary societies in the late 1860s and 1870s. The victory of the Union, as well as the abolition of slavery—which had been viewed by many evangelicals as one of the greatest evils in their society—was a confirmation for many northern Protestants that God's will could be enacted on earth. Moreover, a significant number of Civil War–era women remained unmarried as a result of the war's devastating toll on the population of marriageable young men. These women were looking for meaningful paths to follow and a respectable means of livelihood. Like Elizabeth Russell, 60 percent of the first generation of WFMS missionaries came of age during the Civil War era; all had attended a female seminary or Methodist coeducational college; most were trained as teachers; and the majority reported having had an experience of sanctification and holiness (Robert 1996, 148). With the Civil War behind them and American slavery abolished, many activist-oriented evangelical women were ready for a new call to action.

Leaders of the women's foreign mission movement were able to grasp the moment, channeling this energy into the cause of missions. Launching their foreign missionary society only a few years after the end of the Civil War, leaders of the WFMS wrote in the first issue of *The Heathen Woman's Friend* that "the efforts of our sex during our late war exhibited, as never before, their latent and unemployed power to plan and labor for great and noble ends. These labors being now so happily terminated, Providence has freed our hands for new and yet grander undertakings" (1869, 1, no. 1:2).

For many, the foreign mission movement was the new abolition movement of the day, as they believed that women in the "bonds of heathendom" were like slaves. The missionary periodicals of the northern denominations urged white women to continue to work against women's slavery around the world. The second issue of *The Heathen Woman's Friend* informed the women of the Methodist Episcopal Church that "[a]lmost universally, the bearing of the [Hindu] wife is that of complete subjection and subserviency,—that of an abject menial. . . . The same degradation and social oppression exists among Mohammedan women; they are also *slaves*. . . . It is a fact, that every Christian woman should bear in mind, that no less than 300,000,000 of women are still in the condition of slavery" (WFMS, *HWF*, 1869, 1, no. 2:9, 10; emphasis in original). Now that the work against slavery in the United States was technically over, a whole world of "slaves" was waiting for the saving influence of Christian women. Continuing the tone of many white leaders of the abolition movement, WFMS women combined their outrage over oppression with a hefty dose of paternalism. "God has put a new work in the hands of the women of the Methodist church," proclaimed another issue of *The Heathen Woman's Friend*. "He has committed to our care millions of our dusky sisters. . . . The sick, the ignorant, the degraded, the helpless, stretch out their hands to us who are rejoicing in the light and glory of our Christian civilization. . . . Shall we be deaf to the cry of thousands? Shall we be preoccupied and careless, when God in answer to our prayers has opened to us such precious opportunities of extending His kingdom?" (1873, 4, no. 11:461).

The Heathen Woman's Friend reminded readers not to repeat the mistake of letting slavery go unabated, stating, "Before the war, we assented carelessly to the horrid things that crept into the papers about the abominations of slavery. We dozed off to sleep over its catalogues of cruelty. But when a hunted fugitive looked in at the kitchen door, reaching a branded hand for help, and showing the marks of the bloodhound's teeth, we began to *feel* their force. These things cut down through our stupidity, and touched our hearts" (1869, 1, no. 4:30).

The Heathen Woman's Friend urged women to join local chapters of the WFMS and keep up with the organization's literature, which would keep them focused on "the hard, ugly facts about the lying, thieving, and women-flogging, the licentiousness and infanticide of all pagandom" (1869, 1, no. 4:30). Leaders of the mission movement gave the impression that one would be hard pressed to find any woman outside of the Protestant West who lived a happy life. The early publications of the WFMS presented a nearly monolithic portrayal of women in non-Christian lands: universally oppressed and without the means to save themselves. The task of their salvation was placed squarely on the shoulders of Western women, a burden evangelical women took upon themselves with exhilarating displays of strength and confidence. Postmillennialist hopes melded with imperialist fervor in the early days of women's missions, a marriage that broadened white women's horizons like never before.

4

"Opened Before Our Delighted Vision"

American Protestant Missionaries in New Japan

> This is the undisputed tendency of the modern age—that nations are coming closer and closer in touch one with another, and whoever refuses to join in the union is doomed not only to decay but to destruction.
>
> —Professor Inazō Nitobe
> *Fifty Years of New Japan*, 1909

> These beautiful islands, these gems of the sea, are opened before our delighted vision. . . . I do not yet know all about Japan, but I am greatly astonished by what I have seen thus far. . . . Shall Christianity keep pace with the march of Western civilization in this empire?
>
> —Lucy Ing, missionary, 1875

> Those whom we despised as barbarians are now our teachers in every thing.
>
> —Elderly Japanese man, late 1880s

When Elizabeth Russell sailed for Japan in 1879, as she later wrote in her journal, she "knew nothing of Japan save that it was a little spot on the map near Asia." It was a destination for which she had no time to prepare, as she had learned of her final mission post only a couple of weeks before her trip. She knew nothing of Commodore Perry's famous trip to Japan in 1853, the subsequent signing of the unequal treaties between the United States and Japan, the Meiji Restoration of 1868, or that

Christian mission work in Japan had been legal for only six years when she arrived. She was also unaware that Nagasaki—her final destination—was still considered by missionaries in Japan to be one of the most difficult areas in the country in which to conduct mission work.

Russell and her WFMS companion, Jennie Gheer, first set eyes on Japan "after a tempestuous voyage" of three weeks, when the *Gaelic* landed in Yokohama on Sunday, November 16, 1879. They then transferred to a "little coasting steamer" and, as Russell wrote in her journal, "had a delightful passage along the coast and through the inland Sea of Japan, reaching Nagasaki on Sunday November 23rd." Russell experienced a rush of euphoria at arriving in this land, which Westerners very often found to be wonderfully exotic. "The hills made us both feel at home, but the bay—we had never seen anything so charming," she wrote. "Everything was so novel—the dress, the language and all." Russell and Gheer received a warm welcome from Reverend Davison, who had been responsible for their assignment to Japan, and they stayed with the Davison family while setting up a home for the two of them to share. The Davisons took them to a Thanksgiving dinner at the American Consulate, where they were introduced to elite Americans involved in political and business interests in Nagasaki.

Soon after, the hard realities of their new situation set in. Determined to fulfill their mission assignment, a week after their arrival in Nagasaki Russell and Gheer opened a school with one pupil. The only person they were able to recruit was a Christian convert who wanted to become a Bible woman, the euphemistic title Protestant missionaries gave native women who in practice worked as itinerant preachers (see Robert 1996, 167). This pupil, Ono San (Miss Ono), ended up being more of a teacher for Russell and Gheer than they were for her. Missionaries in Nagasaki at this time had difficulty in finding Japanese people who were willing to teach them the language, and Russell regularly turned to her student for assistance. After a month, Russell wrote that there were "no symptoms of increase in the school."

Russell was startled by the difficult environment she encountered as she struggled to develop a school for people who seemed to want nothing to do with her. "I had expected a cordial reception from the Japanese but had not had it," Russell wrote when reminiscing about her discouragement during her initial months in Japan. Realizing that such "general and deep seated hatred of foreigners and of Christianity surely had some foundation," she began reading about the history of Japan and asking other foreigners why she was having such a difficult time attracting students and finding a personal tutor. It was only then that she learned that Christianity had been banned in Japan for over two and a half centuries before her arrival. Soon concluding that Nagasaki was not "fertile ground" for establishing a mission school, Russell asked Davison why he had sent for her and Gheer. Russell quotes Davison as responding, "Oh . . . I thought I would try one thing more" (Russell, "Pioneer Days").

So Russell and Gheer carried on, and after a month of working with their sole student, they began looking for the perfect name for their school. One of Davison's theological students suggested that they name the school "Kwatsu Sui," meaning "fountain of living waters." They shortened the phrase to Kwassui, and the official name of the school became "Kwassui Jo Gakkō," or Kwassui Female School. Despite the inauspicious beginning of their school, rapidly changing political and cultural forces in Japan would soon begin to work in their favor.

Encountering Meiji Japan

For most Americans who were sent overseas as missionaries in the nineteenth century, arriving at their assigned mission post was their first encounter with a foreign culture, as it was for Elizabeth Russell. Without the ability to return home easily, they were required to engage with the new culture for years on end, coming to terms with the language and the particular social and political climate of their new home. For missionaries who were assigned to Japan in the late nineteenth century, their work required constant revision of their ideological assumptions and mission strategies, as the Japanese government continuously initiated radical changes to modernize the country—a process not always readily embraced by the population at large, but one that ultimately led to the successful restructuring of the country into an imperialist powerhouse in its own right.

This period of rapid change was characterized by numerous reversals and modifications of Japanese policies and attitudes regarding Westerners, as the country negotiated multiple national and international challenges. A long history of national seclusion—a period lasting from the 1630s until the 1850s, during which most foreigners were not allowed to enter Japan and Japanese were not allowed to leave the country—gave way to all-out government attempts to Westernize the country after the Meiji Restoration of 1868. This period of open Westernization was interpreted by many missionaries as a sign that Japan would become a Christian country as it modernized, since they believed that Christianity was inseparably intertwined with the success of modern nation-states. By the 1890s, however, growing Japanese cynicism about the ostensible benefits of wholesale Westernization and a new confidence in Japan's ability to thrive in the age of imperialism strengthened a nativist reverence for traditional Japan, which was a crisis for Protestant missions.

Although there were dramatic shifts in the way Western ideologies and institutions were approached, the logic for these appropriations and rejections was always about remaining free of direct Western control. The creation of a powerful state with a nationalistic citizenry was the central motivating factor of official policy during the Meiji period (1868–1912), as the Japanese government was intent on creating and maintaining "a powerful, wealthy, and autonomous Japanese nation" (Najita 1974, 70).

When Russell came to Japan in 1879, the Meiji government's Westernization agenda had not yet been fully accepted by the populace at large. Preceding her arrival, Methodist missionaries had been working in the country for six difficult years; Protestant missions in general, which had been established in Japan twenty years before Russell's arrival, had experienced a painfully slow beginning. After the Japanese government signed the unequal treaties with the United States and other Western powers in the 1850s—which opened up selected port cities to foreign residence—a few brave missionaries ventured to the newly opened country under the guise of teaching English, since the proselytization of Christianity continued to be strictly forbidden until 1873. The Rev. Guido Verbeck, originally from the Netherlands, was one of the first to arrive as a representative of the Reformed (Dutch) Church of America, hoping that his Dutch background would open the way for mission work, as Japan had maintained a trading relationship with the Dutch when it was closed to the rest of the Western world. After his arrival in 1859, however, he discovered that the Japanese were "not at all accessible touching religious matters. When such a subject was mooted in the presence of a Japanese, his hand would almost involuntarily be applied to his throat, to indicate the extreme perilousness of such a topic." Verbeck lamented that missionaries who first went to Japan were "exposed to insult and even to assault. . . . The swaggering *samurai,* armed with two swords, cast many a scowling look at the hated foreigners, whom they would gladly have expelled from their sacred soil" (Cary [1909] 1993, 50). C. Pemberton Hodgson, who served as the first British consul in Nagasaki during the summer of 1859, was more sympathetic to the samurai's perspective; in 1861 he wrote passionately that "Japan has gained nothing, politically, socially, or morally from the Treaties with foreigners. . . . they have been wantonly insulted in their pride, tempted too often to show their courage, and moreover, often treated with contempt by their inferiors, both in manner and respectability. More than half Japan . . . were and are opposed to the Treaties" (Hodgson 1861, xxxi–xxxii).

The signing of these treaties brought Japan's preexisting internal political turmoil to a head in the 1860s, as numerous samurai factions were furious with the Tokugawa rulers who had succumbed to American pressure to open the country, and they concluded that the current rulers were ineffectual in dealing with the West. As a consequence, the Tokugawa shogunate was overthrown, and the Meiji Restoration began in 1868. This was not the end of political unrest, however. Only an elite group of former samurai controlled the centralized oligarchy of the new government, and samurai outside this group had little or no chance of directly participating in politics during early Meiji.

After the Meiji Restoration, revising the unequal treaties and gaining an equal footing with the West became a driving force in Japanese politics until the treaties finally expired in 1899. All too familiar with the Western argument that the Japanese "were not yet sufficiently civilized to join the West on any sort of equal contractual basis," the Meiji government engaged in rapid social engineering to mold the islands of Japan into a competitive nation-state. While many Japanese leaders desired to create and preserve a unique Japanese identity, they were always aware of the surveillance of

"Americans or Europeans who measured Japan against their own personal standards of civilization" (Sievers 1983, 8). The new Meiji leadership declared that its strategy for negotiating more favorable treaties with the West was to convince the Western world that the new Japan—Meiji Japan—had embraced "civilization and enlightenment" by adopting from the West those things that made Western countries so powerful.

In its urgency to modernize Japan, the Meiji government unleashed harsh policies to undermine the power of the samurai and Buddhist priests, as it sought to create a competition-based capitalist economy. The class system of the Tokugawa era was abolished upon the establishment of the Meiji government, and, as a result, nearly three million samurai lost their aristocratic social position and their hereditary stipends and were ordered to shed their "conspicuous symbols of class identification" (Najita 1974, 73). Their lost social status was symbolically marked when they were required to cut off their topknot hair in favor of shorter Western hairstyles and, even worse, to give up their swords. Having been raised during a time when commerce was considered low class and beneath samurai, disempowered samurai were ill-prepared to compete with the merchant class in the developing capitalist market economy. The Meiji government's demands that the populace rapidly discard centuries-old social and economic structures met with resistance, and the hostility that many Japanese felt over the concessions the government was making toward Western powers was often directed toward foreigners in Japan.

In 1871, the Meiji government sponsored the Iwakura Mission, in which leading statesman Iwakura Tomomi—along with other political leaders, ambassadors, specialists, scholars, and students—traveled to the West in order to investigate strategies for treaty negotiations.[1] Members of the expedition studied Western political, economic, military, industrial, and

1. Over one hundred Japanese were sent on the Iwakura Mission. They visited nine major cities in the United States as well as twelve European countries over a period of two years. Their experiences were recorded in a two-thousand-page document, the *Tokumei Zenken Taishi Bei-Ō Kairan Jikki* (A True Account of the Ambassador Extraordinary and Plenipotentiary's Journey of Observation Through the United States of America and Europe), first published in five volumes in 1878 (Kume [1878] 1985).

social institutions in order to determine what Japan needed to appropriate from the West in order to survive as a powerful nation in its own right. Among others, two significant goals for modernizing Japan emerged from the Iwakura Mission: reforming Japanese laws on religion and creating a new educational system. Largely due to its findings, in 1872 the Meiji government created the Gakusei Plan, which outlined its goals for a national public educational system, and in 1873 the government formally lifted the 259-year-old ban on Christianity. Thus, it was largely because of the changes initiated by the Iwakura Mission that Christian missionary activity was able to operate openly in Japan after 1873, particularly in the development of mission schools to supplement Japan's fledgling public educational system.

One of the most important Japanese intellectuals promoting Western education was the bureaucrat Mori Arinori, who formed an elite intellectual society called the Meirokusha to continue the goals of the Iwakura Mission. Its members actively explored how best to borrow ideas and technology from the West, as they believed Westernization was a primary means to Japanese power. The Meirokusha called their project *bummei kaika* (or "Civilization and Enlightenment"—a popular catchphrase of the era), and were successful for some time in silencing critics of their pro-Westernization focus (Shively 1971, 81). There were extreme moments during this period of emulating the West. Some Japanese intellectuals suggested that Christianity be adopted as the national religion, as it was the ideology and spirit of powerful Western nations; Otis Cary states that the Japanese Embassy "had consulted with a German professor of jurisprudence, concerning the expediency of adopting [Christianity] as a state religion," because "[t]hey were anxious to have Japan recognised as on an equality with Western nations, and those who were in Europe saw that the difference in religion added greatly to the difficulty of accomplishing their purpose" ([1909] 1993, 82). In 1884, writer Takahashi Yoshio even proposed that intermarriage with Westerners would strengthen the Japanese race (Shively 1971, 94). Mori himself even considered this idea while touring the West as a member of the Iwakura Mission, but he was advised against it by an American consultant (Rose 1992, 9). While extreme ideas such as these did not last long, a general zeal for Westernization, motivated primarily by the desire to establish an equal footing with Western nations, continued into the 1880s.

As Japan's Meiji era began, missionary societies rushed to meet the challenge of guiding Japan during its first forays into "civilization." The number of Protestant missionaries in Japan more than doubled in 1873, the year the proscription against Christianity was lifted, bringing the number of Protestant missionaries in Japan to eighty-seven (Cary [1909] 1993, 105). This number included five missionary families sent by the General Board of the Methodist Episcopal Church. Robert S. Maclay, superintendent of the Methodist Episcopal mission in Japan, wrote optimistically, "There is unquestionably a most remarkable movement going forward among the Japanese, and one which offers to the Church of Christ an almost unprecedented opportunity to preach the Gospel among those who are ignorant of the great salvation. . . . it is impossible for any one even to set foot on these shores without coming at once in contact with ample evidence of the radical transformation through which Japan is now passing" (MSMEC, Annual Report, 1873, 137).

However, although the Meiji government had announced two strategic goals—to create "national unity and a national identity" and to develop the "projects of modernization and Westernization"—missionaries encountered a situation that was much more complicated than indicated by the official rhetoric of the new government. Even though the early Meiji government, especially after 1873, often saw American missionaries as helpful purveyors of Western knowledge, numerous Japanese continued to be suspicious of the religious motivations of missionary educators, and with good reason. Particularly during their early years in Japan, missionaries viewed mission schools primarily as tools for proselytization rather than education. Three years after his arrival, Julius Soper, who was among the first group of Methodist Episcopal missionaries to arrive in Japan, articulated the indignation missionaries felt over the ambivalent reception they received:

> The work of the Christian missionary in Japan is more difficult than at first we supposed. . . . The circumscribed limits for open and active work, only a small portion of the empire being yet thrown open to foreigners; the uncertain attitude of the Government toward Christianity; the lack of moral backbone in the Japanese character, and their dislike of any thing that savors of foreign dictation and supremacy, whether of Church or

> State; all these, besides other difficulties and hindrances, rise up before the missionary almost mountain high. (Barclay 1957, 670)

The southwestern island of Kyushu—where the Methodist Episcopal mission had sent Reverend Davison and his wife to be the sole representatives of their denomination—was a hotbed of resistance to the new Meiji government and its policies, and thus the population on this island, which included the city of Nagasaki, was even less open to Westernization and Christianity than other areas where missionaries were stationed. Moreover, the persecution of Christians had been most intense in Kyushu during the years when the religion was forbidden, and raids on secret meetings of hidden Christians in the Nagasaki area had continued well into the nineteenth century (Miyazaki 2003, 21). Kyushu missionaries continued to encounter fear and opposition directed toward their religion in the years after the proscription was lifted. As a result, missionaries in Nagasaki had "more formidable difficulties to encounter than those found at the other ports," which they attributed to southwestern Japan's "intractability to central government and . . . stubborn pride and independence" (Barclay 1957, 133, 669).

Three years after the Davisons' arrival, the 1876 Kyushu-based Satsuma rebellion against the new centralized government in Tokyo limited the movement and work of missionaries in the region. During the uprising Davison wrote, "In consequence of this disturbance we have not been able to visit any part of the surrounding country, and have also experienced a great falling off in attendance upon our weekly congregations. . . . the tangible results of our labor have been far short of what we had hoped to see" (Barclay 1957, 688). By the time Elizabeth Russell and Jennie Gheer arrived in 1879, Reverend and Mrs. Davison had sustained only a small congregation and had attracted only a few students, primarily for private lessons in English.

Shifting Attitudes toward Westerners in Japan

By the 1880s, however, many Japanese were beginning to accept that the West had permanently invaded their world. Although missionaries were extremely worried during their early years in Japan about samurai hostility, the Meiji government had managed to suppress armed samurai rebellion by 1877, and declassed samurai were increasingly coming to terms with the need to refocus their efforts to survive in the new Japan. Ultimately, the early Meiji government's enthusiasm for Westernization, combined with American missionary zeal for proselytization, converged into the successful creation of mission schools by the 1880s, and these schools came to be filled with many students from families of the former samurai class.

The 1872 Gakusei Plan, heavily influenced by the U.S. model of public education, reflected the efforts of the early Meiji government to abolish the old fixed-class system in favor of a model based on the Western ideal of a competitive meritocracy. The Gakusei Plan called for the establishment of 53,760 elementary schools, 256 middle schools, and eight universities (Hara 1995, 96). However, this vision far exceeded the government's financial resources and the availability of trained teachers. By 1879, only 52 percent of the planned elementary schools had actually been established, and less than 40 percent of school-aged children—mostly boys—were enrolled (Marshall 1994, 73). As the government did not have the resources to fully actualize the Gakusei Plan, the private sector, particularly Christian educational institutions, helped provide primary education in early Meiji Japan. Furthermore, the government did not come close to meeting the demand for postprimary education, and private schools played a particularly important role in providing secondary education in the 1870s and 1880s. Of all the established middle schools in 1879, 86 percent were private, and many of them were Christian-affiliated (39). Falling far short of its goals for public education during the first decades of the Meiji era, the government conceded great freedom to Christian schools willing to pick up the slack. Mission schools, with their scholarships and English-speaking faculties offering "Western studies," became important fixtures in the early Meiji educational scene.

During this early period of transition, many Japanese families were indeed affected by the overall interest in Westernization and Western-style education among Japanese leaders, and more and more families decided to send their children to mission schools. In particular, discontented samurai began turning to education as a means of finding new positions of power within Meiji Japan. Determined "to restore their status and insure their future in the new world by the use of Western ideas and techniques" (Scheiner 1970, 45), a significant number of former samurai, including women and girls from samurai families, began to study with Westerners and even converted to Christianity. In fact, almost all converts to Christianity during the 1870s were of the former samurai class (8).[2]

Educating Japanese Women

Mission schools for Japanese girls and women were particularly successful during the 1880s, as the political and social ferment of this decade provided an ideal climate for missionaries to gain footholds in the arena of women's education. As part of its program to improve the image of Japan in the West, Meiji officials took a number of steps to soften the widespread perception that women had a low position in Japan. The first Westerners who entered Japan, often assuming that women's status as wives and mothers reflected a country's level of progress and civility, were horrified when they encountered in Japan an environment in which wives and mothers were not idealized as in the Victorian West. Taking note of such criticisms, the Japanese government sent five young girls[3] on the Iwakura Mission and left them in the United States with host families to learn the "profession of ladies." The idea was that this would demonstrate to Western powers their interest in redefining gender roles in a way befitting a "civilized" nation.[4] Moreover, the government mandated in the 1872 Gakusei Plan that girls as well as boys should receive a primary education, and thus the educational ministry seemed to be affirming Western discourses on the importance of educated mothers. Mori Arinori, who ultimately became Japan's minister

2. Scheiner states that by 1879 there were 1,617 Protestant converts and forty-four Protestant churches in Japan (1970, 101).

3. One of the girls on the Iwakura Mission was Tsuda Ume (later Tsuda Umeko), whose father worked closely with Methodist Episcopal missionaries in Japan. Tsuda Umeko became one of the leading women educators of Japan, and in 1901 she founded the women's school now known as Tsuda University.

4. Sievers states that the government's decision to send the girls on the Iwakura Mission was often used "as a convenient example of Japan's progressive attitude toward women in speeches and articles intended for Western consumption" (1983, 13).

of education, had an American adviser on educational issues, Professor David Murray of Rutgers University, who stressed in his correspondence with Mori the importance of female education, stating, "Female education is equally important with male education. . . . The comfort and happiness of home depend largely upon her, and it is the part of wisdom to give her the means of making it refined and cultivated. The care and supervision of children naturally fall into her hands during their most impressionable years, and the guardians of the future men and women of a nation ought, in common prudence, to be well educated" (qtd. in Marshall 1994, 44).

Mori repeatedly paraphrased these sentiments in his advocacy of women's education during early Meiji. Thus, the Gakusei Plan explicitly revealed the government's radical intention to educate females as well as males when it stated, "Henceforth, in the future, there shall be no community among the people as a whole—whether they be noble, samurai, farmer, artisan, merchant, or woman—where there is an uneducated household nor a family with an uneducated person. . . . Parents and guardians should be held at fault if they fail to have a child—whether boy or girl—attend primary school" (Monbusho, *Gakusei 100 nenshi* 2:11, trans. and qtd. in Marshall 1994, 40–41).

At least on the surface, then, official Japanese discourses on women's place in society during the 1870s resembled Western ideals. However, as Sharon Sievers notes, in reality they sought to "enact some policies that could answer Western criticism without actually engaging Japanese women in the sweeping social change of early Meiji" (1983, 10). While the early Meiji government was concerned with its image in the West, there were signs that women were in fact becoming the "repository of 'traditional' values" within the rapidly changing culture (Sievers 1983, 15).[5] For example,

5. This is a reference to Hanna Papanek's article, "Development Planning for Women," in which she states, "In societies that are changing very rapidly, ambiguous signals are presented to women. Fears are often translated into attempts to prevent changes in their roles. They become the repositories of 'traditional' values imputed to them by men in order to reduce the stresses men face. Resistance to women's greater participation in economic and political life may be felt especially strongly among groups most exposed to rapid change and ambivalent about it" (1977, 15).

when women began to bob their hair as men were adopting shorter Western hairstyles, the government responded by making such hairstyles illegal for women, requiring even women with medical conditions necessitating short hair to obtain a government license for cutting their hair (14). Most significantly, as Kathleen Uno has stated, "a vast number of leaders and ordinary Japanese viewed child-rearing and housework in the old manner," and therefore "there was little enthusiasm for girls' education" in early Meiji (1995, 9). Although the Gakusei Plan called for universal primary education, the education of girls ranked low among the financially strapped government's priorities in the 1870s and 1880s. Postprimary education for young women received even less attention, and as late as 1894 only eight public high schools for girls had been established in Japan. Thus, women in late-nineteenth-century Japan had few other options than to attend Christian mission schools for a higher education.

As a result, private mission schools for girls and women were able to develop freely and with very little competition in the 1880s, as there was official sanction for female schools but little carry through in the way of public schools and few governmental rules and regulations for private schools. Mission schools for girls and women rose in popularity during the 1880s, and as they began offering higher levels of education, they also attracted women desiring more than a primary-level education. The Woman's Foreign Missionary Society of the Methodist Episcopal Church, therefore, was able to develop a successful mission in Japan at the very same time that the General Board was setting up its fledgling mission to the country. At times, the General Board missionaries even looked to the WFMS women to lead the way in the new mission field of Japan.

The WFMS, anxious to make its presence felt in Japan from the very start, sent Dora Schoonmaker as its first missionary to Japan in 1874, a year after the first General Board missionaries arrived. It was her work, in fact, that had inspired Reverend Davison in Nagasaki to send a request for some WFMS missionaries to join him on the southwestern island of Kyushu. Although the WFMS had a policy of sending single missionary women in pairs, in its rush to start women's missions in Japan, Schoonmaker had been sent alone to start a mission school for girls in Tokyo. Arriving before the WFMS could come up with sufficient funding even for her solo work,

Schoonmaker found herself living and conducting classes in a Buddhist temple,[6] a living arrangement obtained through the connections of Tsuda Sen, a friend of Methodist Episcopal missionary Julius Soper.[7] Taking full advantage of the metaphorical richness of her situation, Schoonmaker wrote to *The Heathen Woman's Friend:* "My house is a part of an old temple, the other portion of it being still occupied by the priest and his hideous idol,—Christianity in the very den of paganism, attacking it under its own roof" (WFMS, *HWF,* 1876, 8, no. 11:252).

Schoonmaker immediately began making plans to build a boarding school for Japanese girls, setting a precedent for other WFMS missionaries who would come to Japan. Asserting the benefits of a boarding school over a day school for converting Japanese girls, Schoonmaker wrote,

> [I]f [girls and younger women] can be gathered into schools, where the influence of a Christian *home* shall be constantly about them, they will gradually be won to love a religion which offers them such blessed relief from the bondage of the past and such bright hopes for the future. Feeling the necessity of gaining a stronger hold upon my pupils has been the great incentive that has urged me forward to make preparations for beginning a boarding-school. (MSMEC, Annual Report, 1875, 135)

Boarding schools were common in the United States at this time as well; many American women missionaries, including Elizabeth Russell, had attended a boarding school at some point in their lives. Just as the influential American educator Emma Willard had designed Troy Seminary to

6. Losing much of their patronage after the Meiji Restoration, many Buddhist priests and their temples suffered greatly from lack of funds. Buddhist priests often resented the intrusion of Christians in Japan and Christians' adversarial attitudes to the already downtrodden institution of Buddhism. Thus, renting out space in his temple was likely an act of desperation by the priest. Julius Soper alluded to the financial problems of Buddhist priests when he stated, "The owner of the temple, failing to get support from the few who frequented this shrine, gladly rented it to Mr. Tsuda for school purposes. Many of the smaller temples are falling into disuse from lack of funds to support the priests" (MSMEC, Annual Report, 1875, 134).

7. Tsuda Sen was the father of Tsuda Umeko.

be a boarding school "so that her control could be complete" in molding the young women who came through her doors (Scott 1978, 691), missionaries wanted to completely immerse their students in the life of their mission schools (although Troy Seminary and mission schools did enroll day students as well).

The missionaries of the General Board were pleased with Schoonmaker's work; Soper reported that during Schoonmaker's first year "two women . . . Miss Schoonmaker's scholars, gave me their names as candidates for baptism" (MSMEC, Annual Report, 1875, 134). With the initial modest success of Schoonmaker's school in Tokyo, Davison, down in Kyushu, hoped that a similar boarding school for girls would find more success than other missionary efforts up to that point in the "rocky field" of Nagasaki.

Rising Fortunes for Kwassui Jo Gakkō

For Russell and Gheer, who arrived as the first WFMS missionaries in Kyushu, the favorable conditions for their work were not immediately apparent when the 1880s began, as the people of Nagasaki continued to spurn Kwassui Jo Gakkō; nevertheless, despite the chilly reception of the school among Nagasaki families, in February 1880 three girls from the Kyushu city of Kagoshima entered the school as boarders. The school slowly grew to eighteen pupils by the end of the 1880–81 school year, as girls outside of the Nagasaki area trickled in. Russell was pleased when Davison wrote in his 1880 missionary report, "The past year has not been without its signs of substantial encouragement; in fact, we occupy to-day a stand-point from which our future looks brighter than at any former period during our history as a mission. The late additions to our working force have added materially to our prosperity. Misses Russell and Gheer, of the W.F.M.S. of our Church, have done nobly" (WFMS, Annual Report, 1880, 175).

Apparently, Kwassui's moderate enrollment during the 1880–81 school year was all it took for Russell to begin to have grand visions of success. In a relatively unstructured environment, away from the constraints of her own society, Russell was invigorated by the opportunity to reach her full potential as a leader. While Russell and her colleagues were still struggling with the fact that "the people of Nagasaki paid no attention to us," in the summer of 1881 Russell convinced the WFMS to grant her eight thousand dollars to build a large school building for Kwassui. Not only did she begin to make arrangements to build an expensive school building for Japanese girls and women, but she managed to obtain a prime piece of real estate on which the British had originally planned to build their consulate. In her journal, Russell exulted that it was "the most beautiful site I know of for a school." This was no overstatement; it was a site evoking power and prestige (after all, imperial Britain had found it suitable for their planned consulate building). The property was at the top of a large hill, not only overlooking Nagasaki city and the shipyards below, but also towering above the settlement of foreigners, which was itself elevated above the city. As construction on the rather elaborate school building began on this magnificent property, onlookers, both Western and Japanese, felt that its presence was a challenge to the existing social order. The Western community was particularly outraged by this development.

Even Russell's missionary community was uncomfortable and embarrassed by her undertaking. Davison warned that she was going to "have a great big house and nobody in it." Missionaries were nervous about the reaction of the larger Western community to her project, as relations often had been tense between missionaries and those who had come to work in the business and political arenas of Meiji Japan. Many Westerners in Japan disdainfully viewed missionaries as self-righteous intruders who were unnecessarily meddling in Japanese culture; they also believed—probably with good reason—that missionaries felt themselves to be morally superior to Westerners who were involved in the "crass" material restructuring of Japanese economic, political, and military institutions. One example of the disdain for the missionary movement among secular Westerners in Nagasaki was a spoof that circulated among them titled "A Conversation Between a Tailor and His Wife." It featured a poor humble tailor who would not let his wife have boots made for their son so that they could send money to the missionaries in Nagasaki. In this mockery of the mission movement, which Russell indignantly recorded in her journal, the tailor says of his son, "Bob must be glad when he goes barefooted for the sake of participating in the upholding of missionary societies. . . . if I were a boy I would go stark naked if that could help to diminish the horrors and sufferings the poor missionaries have to endure at Nagasaki!"

Not surprisingly, then, Russell's school-building project provided an ideal target for members of the Western community to vent their frustration toward the missionary enterprise. To them, Russell's school represented all that was useless and misspent in missionary work, for it seemed such a misallotment of resources, energy, and time. One foreign Nagasaki businessman expressed this sentiment when he complained to a visiting Methodist Episcopal bishop that "they are wasting a lot of money up there. Our firm offered them a property amply large for all purposes . . . and they refused it and took up that valuable site and are putting up that great building."

In the midst of such criticism, Russell's troubles deepened during a humiliating episode at her school in the fall of 1881. It looked as if the school would completely collapse during a crisis in which the girls ran away from school and had to be tracked down by the Nagasaki police. After they were found, a Kagoshima father came to collect the whole group of Kagoshima girls and took them back home. Feeling "away down in despair," Russell was then astounded when several Nagasaki girls entered the school "directly after" the Kagoshima girls left. Russell later learned that "the Nagasaki people did not care to send their children where the Kagoshima girls were in predominance," for "the Satsuma people residing in Kagoshima were rebels and had rebelled, the war closing in 1878." A regional factionalism of which Russell had been completely unaware had been working against her school, and the departure of the Kagoshima girls turned out to be a positive thing for the school in terms of enrollment, for Nagasaki families began to take an interest in Kwassui after that point.

With this unexpected turn of events, the school continued to operate, and Russell was soon able to avenge herself against her critics. It just so happened that the celebrated American writer and lecturer Joseph Cook was on an English liner passing through the Nagasaki harbor in May 1882, just as her new school building was being completed. Russell boldly invited him to come speak at the dedication ceremony celebrating the opening of Kwassui's new facilities. Cook agreed and gave a speech in which he argued for the value of women's education, commended Russell for her efforts toward that goal, and chastised the Western community for their opposition to Russell's work. For several days afterward there was a flurry of outrage expressed toward both Cook and Russell in Nagasaki's English-language newspaper, *The Rising Sun and Nagasaki Express.* In one letter to the editor, a critic acidly condemned Russell's school when he stated his offense that "Kuwa Tsu Sui (whatever that may mean) Seminary—a pretentious building on Oura Hill, just completed at the expense of an American missionary society, and intended to be devoted to the education of native females—should be erected in the most ostentatiously conspicuous site on this prominent Cape" (June 3, 1882, 2).

However, Russell's vision in building the school did pay off with the attention it received in elite circles of Japanese. Fortunately for Russell, the grand building and location impressed aristocratic Japanese families, and the number of girls enrolled in the school increased dramatically. When the 1882–83 school year began in September, fifty girls were enrolled, and the numbers steadily increased throughout the 1880s. Russell's school was also a beneficiary of good timing, as the rise in popularity of Christian schools throughout Japan occurred at the very time that she opened Kwassui's expansive school grounds. In 1882 Russell stated, "Two years ago no Coolie in Nagasaki, however poor, would send his daughter to our school, because it was Christian; now we have over thirty Nagasaki girls [in addition to girls from other areas], and more coming" (WFMS, Annual Report, 1882, 40). Five years after the new Kwassui school building was opened, the school was so crowded that another wing had to be built onto the original building, and by the end of the decade, the school would have nearly two hundred students (WFMS, Annual Report, 1889, 53). In 1884, Christians in nearby Fukuoka City, inspired by a revival led by a Japanese preacher there, requested that someone from Kwassui come to start a similar girls' school in Fukuoka. Jennie Gheer answered this call and started Fukuoka Jo Gakkō (Fukuoka Girls' School) with an opening enrollment of sixty-seven pupils (WFMS, Annual Report, 1885, 53).

The entire Methodist Episcopal Church was greatly encouraged by the successful work of the WFMS in Japan; Bishop Isaac Wiley summed up the optimism many felt about Japan when he wrote in the 1880s that "there is not in the world another field for missionary and philanthropic effort so hopeful and inviting and so ripe for immediate and glorious harvest as is now offered among the daughters of Japan" (Isham 1936, 240). Until the 1890s, missionary women had heady years of success, during which many of them, including Elizabeth Russell, came to love the country they had adopted as their permanent home. However, they would not always feel so welcome as the century drew to a close in turbulent Meiji Japan.

5

"The World Moves"

Protestant Missionaries Negotiate Gender Ideologies

> Japan is a country of sudden changes. The bright prospects that gave rise to the hope that the country would be speedily evangelised were soon clouded over. . . . The effect of the reactionary movements was speedily felt by the Christian schools and especially by those for the education of girls. Critics declared that the young women in these schools lost their gentle manners, becoming forward, mannish, and proud.
>
> —Otis Cary, *A History of Christianity in Japan*, 1909

When Japan entered a period of Westernization in the 1880s, Americans invested in the development of the country felt tremendous responsibility for instructing Japanese on how to become civilized. By the end of the century, however, Western missionaries would be scrambling to retain a position of any relevance in Japan. Although she took an unconventional path, Elizabeth Russell created a school that would become a model for other WFMS schools in their attempts to survive the rise of Japanese nationalism.

In the first decades of the Meiji period, the Japanese seemed to be complying with Western cultural leadership, as English-speaking teachers were in great demand among those seeking a competitive edge in the new society. Missionaries felt a growing urgency to make sure Christianity came with the package of Westernization, believing disaster would ensue if it did not. As Elizabeth Russell's missionary colleague, the Rev. John C.

Davison, wrote in 1881, "The people are clamoring for higher education, and it is the extremest folly to underrate this fact. . . . Our duty is to meet this thirst for knowledge with Christian teachers and a pure science, thus preventing the Japanese mind from falling into materialism and infidelity" (MSMEC, Annual Report, 1881, 211). Russell embraced the goal of simultaneously civilizing and Christianizing Japan. Stating that "[t]he school is the hope of the Church in Japan," Russell was convinced that exposure to Western education would make the minds of her students fertile ground for Christian conversion. She wrote in 1886,

> My reading, history, arithmetic and algebra classes are all in English, the language of civilization, the language of progress. . . . We look for results not only in the acquisition of a knowledge of these subjects, but in the waking up of powers that would forever lie dormant under the mental enervation that seems to be induced by the continued study of Chinese . . . the teaching of these branches is indirectly religious work and we may look for early results . . . in the students' steadily broadening views on all subjects. (MEC, Minutes of the Woman's Conference, 1886, 25)

Unlike many of her colleagues in the Woman's Foreign Missionary Society, however, Russell did not see the creation of Christian wives and mothers as her central purpose. Russell dreamed of building a school with an advanced level of education like her alma mater, Washington Seminary, and its model, Emma Willard's Troy Female Seminary. From the very beginning, Russell stated that her purpose in Japan was to train her students to become Christian teachers. While Russell was influenced by prevailing Victorian gender ideologies—in that she saw teaching as the primary role for women in the public sphere—the fact that she was more interested in developing Christian teachers than Christian mothers was a divergence from the rhetoric of early women's missionary societies. The WFMS was founded with the goal of transforming the domestic space of foreign lands, and many WFMS missionaries in Japan had a strong commitment to turning Japanese girls into good Christian wives and mothers. While Russell at times displayed her own ethnocentricity in her rhetoric, educationally rigorous private schools like hers would become a magnet for progressive Japanese women.

During the 1890s, as it shifted its national strategy away from overt Westernization, the government would step up efforts to control Christian missionary activity and women's education, as higher education for women came to be strongly associated with the corruptions of the West. Despite much criticism from conservative Japanese, however, Kwassui continued to push ahead with increasingly improved academic courses throughout the 1890s. While this was partly a result of Russell's strategy to compete by raising her school to a higher level than that of government schools, her work was also informed by her own understanding of the purpose of missionary work and education for women.

Russell and the other teachers at Kwassui organized a rigorous educational program for their students, creating a school that far surpassed WFMS plans for developing mission schools that would create efficient Christian mothers and housekeepers. Russell emphasized in her annual reports that Kwassui's academic program included nontraditional subjects for female students seldom taught in either Japan or the United States, such as "physiology and botany, zoology, analysis, and advanced classes in mathematics" (WFMS, Annual Report, 1886, 44). To the displeasure of most everyone involved in Kwassui, she also insisted that her students learn Latin and Greek, subjects that had been adopted by the most progressive women's colleges in the United States in order to gain an equal footing with men's colleges. Thus, in addition to learning English, Kwassui students were required to learn Latin and Greek from English-language textbooks, which meant that they were learning third and fourth languages through a second language. Her successor, Mariana Young (the principal of Kwassui Jo Gakkō from 1897 to 1920), said of Russell, "If she believed she was right, she would push ahead for the goal, no matter how many dissonant voices were about her" (Couch n.d., 8–9).

Through Russell's petitioning, in 1883 the WFMS assigned Miss Emma J. Everding, a graduate from Syracuse University with a degree in science, to teach at Kwassui. Russell worked with Everding to map out a plan to expand Kwassui to include a college-level program and to solicit enough funds from the United States to open a first-rate science department in the school. Largely as a result of Russell's fund-raising ability, Kwassui generated enough interest among missionary supporters to provide their school with "a liberal lot of physical and chemical apparatus sufficient to perform the leading experiments; also a planetarium and a set of anatomical charts." As a result, Kwassui opened its science department in 1885.

Russell not only believed that higher education was important for the women in her school, but she was also convinced that developing a program of higher education would be the most strategic way to respond to the initiatives of the Japanese government. In 1886, the Japanese Education Ministry, led by Mori Arinori, stepped up its efforts to increase enrollment of girls in public primary schools, and Russell saw this as a way to gain WFMS support for her educational agenda. On behalf of the faculty of Kwassui, she announced in her 1886 report to the Woman's Conference, "It is our desire, and we are a unit on this, to make the Nagasaki school one of high grade only. The government of Japan is working with most commendable zeal, to elevate the standard of its primary schools for girls. They are open everywhere, and we would make them feeders to this and other mission schools" (MEC, *Minutes of the Woman's Conference,* 1886, 45).

By the next year, Russell received approval from the WFMS to "raise Kuwassui to the college grade," and the school formally opened its college program in 1888, while continuing to offer a primary course. As a result of Kwassui's advanced program of study, some of the earliest female physicians in Japan were graduates of Russell's school. For example, Dr. Inoue Tomi, who was in the first Kwassui college graduating class of 1889, obtained her medical degree at the University of Michigan, later rising to become the school doctor of the prestigious Peeresses School in Tokyo (Couch n.d., 10).

As the Japanese government systematized its patriarchal agenda for women over the course of the Meiji period and became increasingly critical of female mission schools, Russell became more and more outspoken about women's rights. She urged her Japanese and Western colleagues to work toward an educational system that would diminish the educational gulf between men and women, for she argued, "Whatever leads out the mental powers of man, leads out the mental powers of women, as there is no sex in mind" (MEC, *Minutes of Woman's Annual Conference . . . in South Japan* 1903, 11, 17). While such sentiments drew the ire of conservatives in

Japan, it resonated with the numerous Japanese women who were drawn to her school.

Diverse Agendas among WFMS Schools

Although Russell received formal approval from the WFMS for her progressive school, in the 1870s and 1880s there was no consensus among missionaries on how best to approach women's education, and really no way for missionaries in this period to know what kind of curricula would help their schools survive the rapidly shifting political winds of Meiji Japan. Although the 1872 Gakusei Plan had called for a radically egalitarian primary school system, the 1882 annual report of the Japanese Education Ministry stated, "Girls' high school education should not have the same curriculum as that of the boys. . . . In addition to teaching [girls] the principles of correct behavior, household economy, the nursing of infants, sewing and handicrafts should be part of the curriculum" (Marshall 1994, 72–74). Although this perspective itself had critics among Japanese intellectuals, such as Fukuzawa Yukichi—who stated that "[s]uch education is less than useless"—many Japanese educators loyally supported the view of the Education Ministry. Yet, despite the Education Ministry's focus, in 1884—the year before Kwassui opened its science department—women were permitted to take the government exams required to receive medical licenses (Sievers 1983, 76). While the government in the 1880s stressed that women should retain the characteristics of women in old Japan, it also supported seemingly contradictory policies at times in order to involve women in activities that were of value to the developing state, such as medical or industrial work. Thus, missionaries in the 1880s had multiple interpretations of what kind of girls' school would be the most well received in Japan. More conservative missionaries mistakenly believed Meiji Japan would eventually embrace the Western ideal of "True Womanhood" as part and parcel of Christianity, and would come to see Japanese women as the moral compass of the domestic sphere.

Contrary to missionaries' expectations, however, Meiji-era Japanese discourses on womanhood increasingly focused on what Sharon H. Nolte and Sally Ann Hastings have called the "cult of productivity" (1991, 154, 173). Rather than reigning supreme over the domestic sphere like the idealized

Victorian woman, official Japanese gender ideologies ultimately envisioned the ideal woman as not only laboring selflessly for the family in the domestic sphere (which itself was officially defined as a public, not private, space), but also for the newly conceived "family-state" in the broader arena of the national economy. Japanese leaders thus emphasized the need for female education to focus on industrial education in addition to domestic economy. This limited openness to women's work in the public sphere was not about women's emancipation (in fact, women's rights were severely restricted over the course of the Meiji period); instead, it was about filial piety, or obedience and service to the family-state.

Despite occasional government proclamations regarding appropriate female education, the lack of government regulations for private schools in the 1880s created an environment in which mission schools for girls and women developed a diversity of educational programs, reflecting the range of gender ideologies among the missionaries themselves. During the 1880s, the WFMS of the Methodist Episcopal Church supported six boarding schools and fourteen day schools throughout Japan. At first, many WFMS missionaries believed the most logical approach would be to teach what both Japanese and Americans considered to be womanly subjects, making Russell's school a bit of an anomaly among WFMS schools.[1] For example, missionaries at the WFMS school in Tokyo, which Dora Schoonmaker had founded, stated in their annual mission report that "sewing and cooking are regularly taught, our aim being to make of our girls not only good scholars and able Christian workers, but womanly women who shall by and by be efficient housekeepers, and good wives and mothers" (MEC, Minutes of the Woman's Conference, 1886, 17).

This strategy was repeatedly affirmed by the Woman's Conference of Methodist Episcopal Missionaries in Japan (which included both WFMS

1. The only other mission schools that developed higher-education departments in the 1880s were Ferris Seminary, which was founded in 1870 by Dutch Reformed Church missionary Mary E. Kidder, and Kobe Girls' School, founded in 1875 by missionaries of the American Board of Commissioners for Foreign Missions. Ferris first created a higher-education department in 1882, while Kobe Girls' School initiated its higher-education program in 1885 (see Ishii 2004, 12–13, 110).

missionaries and missionary wives associated with the General Board). In the 1887 minutes of the Woman's Conference, the committee on boarding schools emphasized that the goals of women's mission education was to shape the domestic sphere, stating that since Japanese "have no realization of what constitutes home life in a Christian land . . . women and girls [in mission boarding schools] shall be given not only a Christian education, but thorough instruction in all the principles of Domestic Economy" (MEC, Minutes of the Woman's Conference, 1887, 16). Missionaries in Japan were confident throughout the 1880s that instruction in Western-style housewifery would long continue to be a major attraction for Japanese; the Woman's Conference stated in its 1886 resolutions that "as European customs are being rapidly adopted in Japan, our pupils [should] be taught foreign cooking, foreign sewing and fancy work" (MEC, Minutes of the Woman's Conference, 1886).

Beyond Bible lessons, English classes, and instruction on how to become Western-style housekeepers and mothers, most mission schools were satisfied to provide students with a "Japanese course equal to that of the government schools of a similar grade" (MEC, Minutes of the Woman's Conference, 1886, 17). Only when WFMS mission schools began to receive real competition from Japanese schools in the 1890s and early 1900s did the conference as a whole begin to reconsider this approach, and Russell's Kwassui Jo Gakkō became a model for other WFMS schools.

Early on, however, WFMS schools, whether they desired to create Christian wives and mothers or highly educated Christian professionals, had to come to terms with the fact that their ideals were not possible for many women as a result of the desperate poverty many Japanese faced during the rapid transformation of the country. Mrs. Flora Best Harris, the wife of Methodist Episcopal missionary Merriman Harris, was one of the most outspoken advocates of industrial training for Japanese women; as she stated in one of her letters, "*The imperative need of the hour is new occupations for Japanese women.* . . . [and] Christian industrial schools will help solve the problem of selfsupport" (Araya 1976, 82, emphasis in the original). Russell was the first to add an industrial department to her school in 1886, as "a means of providing many girls with employment . . . in teaching the girls to cut and fit dresses" (WFMS, Annual Report, 1887, 48). In 1887, she joined with Mrs.

Harris in convincing the Woman's Conference of the Methodist Episcopal Japan mission to support the creation of an "Industrial Home for Friendless Women" in Tokyo. By the end of the decade, the WFMS was conducting several industrial programs to train women to work in Japan's growing industries. It was hard to ignore that Japan had an uniquely high participation of women in newly developing industries, averaging around 60 percent of the industrial labor force between 1870 and 1930 (Sievers 1983, 84). Many WFMS missionaries came to realize that providing training in marketable skills for women would make the mission schools themselves marketable, even if they disagreed on how much higher education their schools should provide. Remaining marketable in Japan would continue to modify WFMS ideals for female education for the rest of the century.

The Popular Rights Movement

Regardless of missionaries' agendas, Japanese graduates of mission schools had their own goals, which at times spelled trouble for Christian mission schools. Mission schools often introduced young women, to some extent, to Western liberal ideals of individualism and equality, and numerous Japanese, including women, explicitly incorporated Christian and/or liberal Western philosophy into the rhetoric of their resistance movements against the power of the Meiji government. Graduates of mission schools and Christian converts often supported movements to advance equal rights and political liberty in Meiji Japan, and were on friendly terms with the Freedom and Popular Rights Movement *(Jiyū Minken Undō)*, which sought to pressure the Meiji government to adopt a Western-style democratic form of government. Thus, during the first three decades of the Meiji era, Western ideologies were used in a variety of ways to support the interests of both those seeking to maintain their positions of power and those trying to resist or supplant the developing power structure. When resistance groups became too threatening for the government, conservative Japanese officials often blamed foreign elements in Japan, leading to criticism of Christianity and mission schools for contributing to such subversive activity. In the 1870s and 1880s, the Popular Rights movement, in particular, contributed to the Meiji government's reaction against liberal Western philosophy, women's rights, and Christianity, a conservatism which would reach its peak in the 1890s.

Discontented former samurai began the Popular Rights movement in the 1870s, drawing from Western philosophical notions of natural rights to argue that individuals had an equal right to property and political liberty, and that individuals should not be taxed without political representation. Although the former samurai who led the movement were often themselves quite elitist, Japanese of all classes, including Japanese women, joined the Popular Rights movement to advance their political representation as well. As historian Irokawa Daikichi has noted, the "breakdown of ideas of 'village' and 'household'" and the rise of "elements of capitalism," which coincided with an increasingly systematic state control of everyday life, led to a widespread desire to limit the government's power (1985, 17). While denouncing Shinto, Confucianism, and Buddhism as antagonistic to their liberal politics, Popular Rights activists were on friendly terms with Japanese Christians, as they believed Christianity had an intimate relationship with Western "rationalism and democratic principles" (Honda 1909, 86).

By 1881, Popular Rights activists had pressured the government to agree to develop a constitution and representative diet by 1890. The promise of a representative assembly gave them much hope, and after their victory in 1881, they formed the Liberal Party. Shaken by these concessions and the rise of an opposition political party, the government became even more repressive of political activity as the Meiji oligarchy sought to strengthen its authority before establishing a representative government. The Liberal Party was forced to dissolve by 1884, and in 1887 the Peace Preservation Law was instituted to curtail any further oppositional political activity. This law banned unauthorized assemblies and strengthened the government's control over print media, as it required all newspapers to be censored by authorities. This law would ultimately make Christian meetings and activities more difficult in Japan, along with women's movements to gain political rights.

A number of Japanese were actively involved in seeking political rights for women in the 1870s and 1880s. Many politically radical women had attended Christian mission schools, as these schools were the primary means for women to gain higher education and teaching positions during early Meiji. For example, two of Meiji Japan's most prominent feminists, Kishida Toshiko and Fukuda Hideko, had connections with Christian mission schools at some point in their lives. Kishida began receiving national attention in 1882 when Popular Rights activists put her on a lecture circuit in which she spoke to large audiences about the "overwhelming justice of extending the rights of women." As a teenager, Fukuda was inspired when she heard one of Kishida's speeches and became motivated herself, as she put it, "to smash the corrupt customs of former days relating to women" (Sievers 1983, 36). In her late teens, Fukuda, along with her mother, opened a school for women in 1883, with the belief that women should have better employment opportunities.

The activities of Kishida and Fukuda, like many of the prominent leaders of the Popular Rights movement, were ultimately repressed by the government. In 1883, Kishida was jailed for her harsh criticisms of government policies concerning women and marriage. After her release from prison and the dissolution of the Liberal Party in 1884, Kishida taught at the Reformed Mission's Ferris Seminary in Yokohama (Sievers 1983, 47). Fukuda's school was shut down by the authorities in 1884 when they found her at a Liberal Party gathering, after which Fukuda attended a mission school. She was then jailed in 1885 for her involvement in the Osaka Incident, in which a number of radicals were caught making plans to establish a new government. By association, government officials began to turn against mission schools because of their connection with activist women such as these.

Throughout the Meiji period, the government steadily increased its efforts to place female education on a separate track from that of male education, emphasizing the importance of preserving the "submissiveness and virtuousness of Japanese women" (Marshall 1994, 72–74). Upon the promulgation of the Education Act of 1880, females were formally excluded from public middle schools, and afterward public schools were rarely coeducational from the third year of primary school (Hara 1995, 98–99). In 1882 the government created the blueprint for *kōtō jogakkō* (high[er] girls schools),[2] in which girls would focus on domestic sciences rather

2. The translation of *kōtō jogakkō* as "high[er] girls' schools" indicates that girls' postprimary schools were not at the level of high schools for boys (see Marshall 1994, 74).

than "impractical" subjects such as math and natural sciences. Until the government was able to offer an extensive program of free public education, however, such moves drove more women to attend private Christian schools throughout the 1880s.

Not surprisingly, mission schools with educational programs like Kwassui's received criticism from the government, even as they were becoming popular among Japanese women. Throughout the active period of the Popular Rights movement, the government often blamed mission schools for political dissent among women, stating that they had a "wrong view" of girls' education and were destroying Japanese women's ability to submissively fulfill their duties in the household and larger society. In the 1880s the Ministry of Education and government-sponsored newspapers pronounced that many private institutions that focused on women's education, especially mission schools, were "responsible for vanity . . . and lack of refinement in the young women" and produced "the modern girl . . . [who] has almost transformed herself into a man" (Burton 1914, 66).

Japanese Conservatism in the 1890s

When the Meiji Constitution was finalized in 1889, a new level of political conservatism enveloped Japan, which ultimately led to a crisis for mission schools. Mission schools were now compelled to respond and adapt to dramatic changes in Japanese politics and nationalism, signaled throughout the 1890s by the advent of the 1890 Imperial Rescript on Education, the conclusion of the treaty revisions in 1894 (which went into effect in 1899), the Sino-Japanese War of 1894–95, the Meiji Civil Code of 1898, and increasingly restrictive educational ordinances. Interconnected with these developments was Japan's shifting political focus from overt borrowing from the West to a nativist pride in Japanese accomplishments and abilities.

Even before the 1890s, a number of leading Japanese had agitated against the pro-Western direction of the Meiji government, and their oppositional stance became more powerful as attempts to revise the unequal treaties with the West repeatedly failed. Eventually, even those who had strongly advocated a pro-Western approach became disillusioned, as it became apparent to them that attempts at Westernization had not significantly changed the attitudes of Western powers toward Japan (Pierson 1980). Japanese officials during early Meiji had expected that treaty revisions would be successful by 1887, and thus, "in order to secure the smooth passage of this revised draft, the Government did everything possible to clothe the people with the garments of Western civilization" (Honda 1909, 89). However, when this attempt at treaty revision failed, much of the enthusiasm for Westernization quickly diminished. Mori Arinori, who had been one of the leading proponents of the Westernization strategy, was assassinated in 1889, on the day the Meiji Constitution was promulgated,[3] which dramatically symbolized the country's shift from intensely focusing on Westernization as the path to national power to focusing on Japanization for the sake of national power. Nativists and Confucianists, whose voices had been suppressed by the prevailing government enthusiasm for Western borrowing in the 1870s and 1880s, took advantage of the growing antipathy to the West to openly critique the appropriation of Western ideologies as anti-Japanese (Gluck 1985, 114).

Motoda Eifu, a Confucianist palace adviser, was particularly significant in redirecting Japan toward a focus on filial piety and nationalism. Motoda had continually opposed the policies of the pro-Western faction of the Meiji government, asserting that officials such as Mori Arinori were trying to "convert Japanese into facsimiles of Europeans and Americans" (Marshall 1994, 54). After Mori's assassination, Motoda was able to redirect the focus of national education into a more conservative Confucian-based program and was influential in the creation of the 1890 Imperial Rescript on Education, which stressed that reverence for the emperor should be instilled in schoolchildren.

When the long-awaited revision of the unequal treaties occurred in 1894, it did not change the nativist emphasis of the government. Its terms raised much concern among Japanese, for when the new treaties would take effect in 1899, foreigners would no longer be required to reside only

3. Otis Cary states that Mori was assassinated "because of an act of irreverence that he was alleged to have committed some time before by lifting with his walking-stick the curtain that hung before the holy place in the great Shinto shrine at Ise" ([1909] 1993, 214). Mori's assassin saw this as a sign of disrespect to the Shintoist Imperial throne.

in designated port cities; thus the treaties would usher in a new era of "mixed residence" with foreigners. This gave rise to even more efforts to create a strong Japanese identity in order to resist Western influences, and the government became more focused than ever on instilling the "civil morality" of imperial reverence and filial piety among Japanese citizens. This drive to create a nationalistic citizenry was further intensified during the Sino-Japanese War of 1894–95.

No publication of the day provided more in-depth analyses of the effects of these developments on mission schools than *The Japan Evangelist*, a Christian periodical that began publication in 1893. Throughout the momentous events of the 1890s, *The Japan Evangelist* chronicled national events in politics, religion, and education, and featured the commentaries of leading Japanese Christians as well as Westerners.[4] In 1893—before most mission schools had adequately digested the significance of the changing sentiments of Japanese leaders toward Christianity—contributor Rev. A. Miyake stated that

> up to the year 1889, I should say Christianity was at the stage of welcome. . . . But action and reaction come alternately in the course of nature, so the general feature of Japanese thought began to change towards conservatism from the year when the first parliament was called. . . . We are not yet out of the depth of this trouble. All schools founded on Christian principles are thinned out to the half, third, and even to the fifth part of the number they registered at their high prosperity. . . . Surely Christianity and the Christian Church in Japan have entered into the . . . stage of severe trial and criticism. (1893, 1, no. 1:54)

The Meiji Constitution and Imperial Rescript on Education

A number of missionaries in Japan had been enthusiastic about the promulgation of the Meiji Constitution in 1889, particularly because it explicitly made religious freedom the law of the land. Almost immediately after the

4. The introductory publication proclaimed that "in these pages the Japanese, as far as possible, shall speak for the Japanese and of the Japanese" (*Japan Evangelist* 1893, 1, no. 1:5).

constitution went into effect, however, missionaries began to encounter new difficulties. It quickly became apparent that Japanese officials who had opposed the introduction of Christianity into Japan found the religious freedom clause to be a useful tool for condemning Christian activity in educational institutions. As Carol Gluck states, "Article 28 of the Constitution . . . guaranteed that Japanese subjects should enjoy freedom of religion, 'within limits not prejudicial to peace and order, and not antagonistic to their duties as subjects.' Yet in the course of the decade Christianity was deemed incompatible with loyalty, and on that basis religion in the schools declared unconstitutional" (1985, 57).

Opponents of Christianity were also able to cast Christian schools in a negative light through their use of the 1890 Imperial Rescript on Education. While the constitution made the powers of the emperor "legally explicit for the first time in Japanese history" (Gluck 1985, 76), the Rescript on Education used this newly defined imperial power to reinstate Shintoist and Confucian morality based on reverence for the emperor and filial piety.

The 1891 "Les Mageste Incident" provided the ammunition nativists needed to highlight the incompatibility of Christianity with imperial reverence. In this scandal, Christian educator Uchimura Kanzō refused to bow before the imperial seal on the Rescript on Education at a school assembly.[5] Soon after this incident, Imperial University professor Inoue Tetsujirō published a widely read attack on Christianity, titled "On the Conflict between Religion and Education." He argued that Christianity detracted from government attempts to foster nationalism because it was a foreign ideology that demanded obedience to a universal God as opposed to the Japanese emperor. He stated that "monotheism is like an absolute monarchy," and thus "the two powers, the Rescript and Christianity are not in harmony" (qtd. in Cary [1909] 1993, 243). Uchimura and other Japanese Christians argued that Christianity *was* compatible with Japanese nationalism; Uchimura said that his life was dominated by his love for the two Js: Jesus and Japan. Partly resulting from this incident, Uchimura founded the Nonchurch movement, which stressed independence from Western

5. Uchimura lost his teaching post as a result of this action.

missionaries and the importance of making Christianity a religion that was compatible with being a patriotic Japanese (Miura 1996). Gluck states that between "Uchimura's refusal to bow in 1891 and the beginning of the Sino-Japanese War in 1894, 76 volumes and 493 articles appeared that argued the case for and against the loyalty of Christians" (1985, 133). Under pressure from the government, Japanese Christians began to distance themselves from Western missionaries in order to show their loyalty to Japan.

Shifting Gender Ideologies, 1889–1899

The growing conservatism and nationalism had heavy consequences for women in Japan, in addition to Christians. According to Sharon Sievers, after Mori's assassination in 1889, "the Education Ministry was dominated by men who had never agreed that women should exercise more power in the family" (1983, 108). Thus, in addition to their Christian focus, the "cult of domesticity" undergirding Western mission schools for girls and women, with its ideology of women's moral and religious leadership in the home, was increasingly called into question in the 1890s.

When Mori had been the minister of education in the 1880s, he had been sympathetic to the Western understanding of true womanhood and women's education. After his death, however, the new minister of education, Ōki Takatō, pronounced that girls' education should not threaten "their chastity and beautiful manners" (qtd. in Marshall 1994, 74)—and more than ever mission schools were targeted as presenting that very threat. The Western domestic ideal included a focus on marriage based on romantic love, rather than arranged marriages. The new leaders of education in Japan saw such Western ideals as a threat to female morality, which they defined as selfless obedience to the family. As a result, "Christians were on the defensive in the 1890s, attacked by those who saw in Christian higher schools for women a source of encouragement of sexual license" (Sievers 1983, 108).

Not only was the Western cult of domesticity challenged, but mission schools that provided education beyond the domestic ideals of their own mission societies were also continually called into question. Even some Japanese Christians, such as *Japan Evangelist* contributor Reverend Miyake, harshly criticized the higher education provided by some Christian schools for girls and women. Despite the fact that many mission schools for girls and women *did* focus on domestic economy, he proclaimed that they were still deficient in this area:

> A severe criticism, which the public often makes on female education in Japan is that intellectual attainments tend to make the girls gradually lose the quality of modesty. . . . Girls, before and above other intellectual pursuits, must learn the practical art of house-keeping. . . .
>
> In our Christian schools, the sciences and languages were and still are principally taught, with altogether too little training for domestic life. Public criticism of graduates from these schools on the ground that they know nothing about sewing, cooking and house-keeping caused female education to become very unpopular. (*Japan Evangelist* 1895, 2, no. 3:161–62)

As Japanese officials became more interested in controlling women's education, the 1890s saw an increase of government-funded higher women's schools, or *kōtō jogakkō* (Marshall 1994, 74). *Kōtō jogakkō* aimed to "develop in young women refined taste and gentle and modest character," providing middle-class women "enough education—but no more than necessary—to fulfill their duties within the home" (Nolte and Hastings 1991, 158).

The government's interest in women's service to the family and state was heightened by the Sino-Japanese War. Women's patriotic activities during the war, such as volunteer societies providing war relief, thoroughly convinced the Japanese government of the value of women in developing a powerful and expansionist nation. In discussing the aftereffects of the Sino-Japanese War, *Japan Evangelist* contributor C. Nakamura revealed this new appreciation for women's labor when he stated, "Since the War, the number of our factories has been trebled or quadrupled, and as a consequence, many of our women have come to be employed by them, which, in turn, has raised the wages of domestic maids to a great extent. Besides, women physicians, teachers, nurses, bank officers, post and telephone experts, etc., are now greatly needed." In addition to the waged labor of women, Nakamura went on to say that Japanese officials had come to see women as important social contributors in the familial sphere: "The recent

War has proved that educated women are far better, as faithful wives and good mothers, than those who have no education. Owing to this and several other reasons the interest of the people in female education has been greatly awakened" (1897, 4, no. 1:101, 103).

The official Japanese ideal of the educated woman after the Sino-Japanese War was quite different than the Western notion of women as moral leaders in the private sphere. The ideal Japanese woman was obedient to her immediate family as well as to the family-state, and this ideal of obedience was often envisioned in terms of women's labor outside the home. As Kathleen Uno has pointed out (1995), official gender ideologies developed as they did partly because the Japanese government was trying to catch up to other Western powers, and it could not afford to spare the labor of Japanese women; thus the gender ideology called for women's productivity, rather than focusing solely on women's reproductive activity as in Western gender ideologies. However, since the domestic sphere and the public sphere were becoming increasingly separated through industrialization—and thus many families no longer worked together—women were increasingly becoming the primary caretakers of children. While official ideology adjusted to this reality, the government was intent on controlling women's mothering activities as much as possible, for women were not seen as having innately superior abilities in child rearing. Thus, in the 1890s there was a "growing effort to control women's education and use it as a vehicle for state social policy" (Sievers 1983, 108).

While the government provided more educational opportunities for women as the nineteenth century drew to a close, Japanese leaders' intentions for women to remain subordinate members of both the private and public spheres was made evident in the 1898 Meiji Civil Code, which revived the patriarchal *ie* (household) system of the Tokugawa era, legally codifying the male head-of-household's powers over other household members. In the Meiji civil code, as Sievers explains,

> only men were legally recognized persons. Married women were not able to bring legal action independently; they were classified in the same category as the "deformed and the mentally incompetent" in the code. . . . The stipulation that all property would be inherited by the oldest son not

> only did away with the diversity of custom practiced since Tokugawa; it made it impossible for women to be thought of as anything but commodities in a continuing patriarchal, patrilineal market. (1983, 111)

Women's Responses to Conservative Gender Ideologies

Women's rights supporters who had hoped that the new code would give women more, not fewer, civil rights were devastated, as this was one of the most repressive legal documents toward women in Japanese history. It also made clear in no uncertain terms that the government's agenda for women at the end of the century did not include the ideals of the Western "cult of True Womanhood," which the WFMS had sought to transplant to Japan.

Many women in Japan, both Western and Japanese, passionately criticized government policies toward women in the 1890s, including Elizabeth Russell. *The Japan Evangelist* featured articles by a number of Japanese women who assertively opposed the growing repressive tendencies of the government. The regular feature titled "Woman's Department," particularly while it was edited by Iwamoto Kashi from 1894 until her death in 1896, presented views of leading Japanese women of the day, including articles by the prominent women's educator Tsuda Umeko. Iwamoto's own writings provided an important perspective to her English-language audience during the war years, as she critically analyzed the work of missionaries as well as the activities of the Japanese government from the position of a Japanese Christian woman.[6]

While Reverend Miyake's article in *The Japan Evangelist* had called for conformity to the government's developing gender ideologies, Iwamoto

6. Iwamoto Kashi was the first graduate of Ferris Seminary, the first female mission school in Japan. After graduating, she taught at Ferris until her marriage to Iwamoto Yoshiharu in 1889, and she became a well-known writer and translator under the name Wakamatsu Shizuko. Mourning her premature death at age thirty-two, in 1896, *The Japan Evangelist* editors stated that "[t]o the world of literary culture, and to the kingdom of Christ in Japan, her death is an unspeakable loss. She was God's chosen vessel to bear His best gifts to her country-women" (1896, 3, no. 4:230).

boldly countered such conservatism by printing a translation of an article from *Jogaku Zasshi*, a women's educational magazine founded by her husband, which stated that "[a]ll who desire to keep woman in the same narrowed position which she occupied before cannot but be men who do not wish for the true companionship and help of woman, and who have yet to learn the true relation of man and woman" (1895, 2, no. 3:163).

Iwamoto also printed an article by Takaguchi Mika, who used Christian language to argue for women's equality. Takaguchi stated, "It is evident the Creator is not satisfied with woman's doing only domestic work; for He has given her talents for other things also. . . . woman should study and work according to her gifts; for God has given each person a peculiar genius. . . . Woman . . . [y]ou are not a being that should be treated like a machine. . . . you may study and work as far as your strength will permit and as far as your genius can reach" (*The Japan Evangelist* 1894, 2, no. 1:48).

While critiquing conservative Japanese views on women, Iwamoto also called on missionaries to change their often arrogant attitudes toward Japanese perspectives. During a time when many missionaries seemed startled that Japanese were not embracing the West and Christianity, Iwamoto apparently decided that it would be useful to begin her very first "Woman's Department" feature by emphasizing that if missionaries truly wanted to avoid opposition to their work, they needed to change their top-down strategy in converting Japanese. Calling missionaries to work more "graciously" in Japan, she pointed out that missionaries "must not begin by offending [the Japanese] by looking upon them as heathens and consequently a subject to be given lessons in the first elements of morality." Instead, she suggested, it was the missionaries who must be students, as they "will have to understand the extent of their knowledge and ignorance—see with their eyes and hear with their ears. . . . They need first to study and appreciate [the Japanese] cherished moral standard which has hitherto guided their lives" (*The Japan Evangelist* 1894, 1, no. 6:330).

In 1897, *Japan Evangelist* contributor Clara Parrish apparently tried to follow this advice to some extent, although in a conservative way that Iwamoto would not necessarily have appreciated. Parrish combined both the usual arguments for women's education used by nineteenth-century Western women with what she perceived to be the best strategies for convincing

Japanese men of the value of women's academic education. Apparently attempting to address what she saw of Japanese marriage relations, Parrish stressed that educated women would *serve* men better than noneducated women. Parrish thus argued for women's academic schooling by stating, "Man need not fear to make woman the sharer of his dearest hopes and joys. A womanhood educated in the truest sense would not only prepare food for the material man, but would stimulate his mental and moral faculties as well, and would cherish the interests of his home." In the same article, Parrish also evoked the growing late-nineteenth-century Japanese interest in racial improvement by stating, "A careful study of the subject of heredity has proved that it is from the mother that the child receives its courage and its brain power. If a scholarly man is anxious his offspring shall possess talents equal to, or superior to his own . . . he must see to it that he chooses, not so much the fairest flower in all the 'rosebud garden of girls,' but the strongest intellectually and morally" (1897, 4, no. 8:255).

Perhaps most representative of Western women's responses to Japanese gender ideologies was Alice Bacon's *Japanese Girls and Women* (1891), a book she authored with the help of educator Tsuda Umeko. Bacon held fast to the Western belief that unless Japan adopted the gender ideologies of the Christian West, it would never enter civilization. Although Bacon admired the quiet, considerate, industrious, self-deprecating "nature" of the Japanese woman (15), she stressed that as long as Japanese women remained "pinched, nipped, and strangulated, rather like a bonsai" by restrictive Japanese society, so too would the nation's progress be stunted (Rose 1992, 85) Bacon critiqued the Confucian family hierarchy, which she contrasted with Western gender/domestic ideals, stating that the Japanese did not have "the idea of the strong man considering the weak woman . . . but [instead] it is the less important waiting upon the more important, the servant deferring to her master" (1891, 75). Reflecting a common argument of nineteenth-century white American feminists, she compared Japanese women to "the negroes. . . . [i]n the old slave times in the South." Although Japanese women, like slaves, had been "fed and cared for," Bacon argued, they were "at the mercy of men who too often thought only of themselves, and not of the human bodies and souls over which they had unlimited power" (97). Decrying the fact that a Japanese wife must provide her husband "services that a European expects of his valet," Bacon argued that it was not natural for middle- and upper-class Japanese women to have roles similar to those of servants and slaves in their own households. "Even the Empress herself," she declared, "is not exempt from these duties of personal service, but must wait upon her husband in various ways" (76–77). According to Bacon, until middle-class women were thought of "as individuals, with minds and souls to be trained and developed to their highest possibilities," and until "the position of the wife and mother in Japan is improved and made secure, little permanence can be expected in the progress of the nation toward what is best and highest in the Western civilization" (301, 97).

Elizabeth Russell also joined the voices of protest against the Meiji government's suppression of women's political and educational rights. By 1900, she had become an open advocate of women's rights, and she applauded the women's-rights movements in both Japan and the United States. Linking women's work in education with women's emancipation, she urged women not to accept their subordinate status, stating, "before woman in any land rises, she must herself take the initiative, she must show some appreciation of her condition and seek to rise. . . . until a sufficient number of any class show a disposition to rise, they will not rise. Read history in every land; the rich, the great, the powerful, have never voluntarily reached down to lift up the poor, the weak, the lowly" (MEC, *Minutes of Woman's Annual Conference . . . in South Japan*, Fifth Session, 1903, 11, 17). With her feminist sensibility, Russell remained steadfast in her determination to provide a high-level education at Kwassui, even when it was far from clear that this strategy would keep her school alive.

WFMS Responses to Political Changes

After several years of rapid growth, Kwassui's enrollment declined from 190 students in 1889 to 176 students in 1890, and then fell to 134 students in 1891. Russell described the newly developing opposition to mission school education in a personal and graphic way in her 1890 report to the WFMS. Noting that "the Emperor of Japan changed the form of government from an absolute to a constitutional monarchy," she proceeded to discuss the drop in Kwassui's enrollment and described the struggles of one of her Christian students whose family opposed her continued enrollment in a Christian school. Reflecting the sentiments of most missionaries at this time, Russell explained the decline in Kwassui's enrollment in terms of "the anti-foreign feeling prevalent." Immediately following this comment, Russell recounted a dramatic story of a Kwassui student who suffered physical abuse from her family for converting to Christianity. According to Russell, when the teachers "appealed to the law . . . the Judge told them, 'She is only a woman, and Japan has no protection for her. She is under the power of her father—then her husband—then her first born son, and dares not say either her soul or her body is her own'" (WFMS, Annual Report, 1890, 43, 44).

Despite criticism of mission schools' improper education for girls and women, Russell responded to new trends in Japan during the 1890s by further increasing the educational level and rigor of Kwassui, all the while espousing a more overt rhetoric of women's emancipation resembling that of women's rights supporters.

In general, however, during the 1890s the primary strategy of the Woman's Conference of the Methodist Episcopal Church in Japan was to attempt to reconcile its understanding of womanhood with the Japanese government's growing emphasis on domestic training for women, rather than raise the standards of mission schools. While Russell advocated raising the level of mission schools to the highest standard, the WFMS as a whole preferred a path of increasing accommodation to conservative Japanese gender ideals. While this strategy was fairly successful in the short run, in the long run it ultimately proved to be less effective than Russell's educational strategy.

The WFMS schools in Hakodate and Tokyo, which were two of the most successful WFMS schools other than Kwassui, maintained satisfactory enrollments during the 1890s through adding Japanese-focused industrial courses as well as courses such as etiquette and flower-arranging, which were designed to teach students how to be traditional Japanese women. While the Woman's Conference continued to stress its ideals of Christian-centered mission school education, in the early 1890s the Woman's Conference began to deemphasize American-style education. While only a few years before, in light of the Westernization craze of the 1880s, the

WFMS had confidently advocated a program of study emphasizing American-style education and Western subjects of study, by 1891 the WFMS was compelled to resolve that, "in view of the change in sentiment among the Japanese in regard to the study of English . . . the amount of English taught in our schools should be diminished, as soon as practicable" (MEC, Minutes of the Woman's Conference, 1891, 21).

While missionaries at the Hakodate and Tokyo schools accommodated the rising nationalism of the 1890s, most of them continued to believe that the purpose of their schools was to change only one thing in Japan: the religious and moral influence of the woman in the domestic sphere. Not understanding the ways in which official Japanese gender ideology was developing differently from their own, later in the decade they reported with some surprise that when the WFMS boarding schools developed industrial departments, this activity drew "support from high circles, where one might expect to encounter opposition" (WFMS, Annual Report, 1898, 255–56). Although they were compelled to adopt courses of study that seemed adverse to their own gender ideologies in order to stay in business, many of the Hakodate and Tokyo school missionaries were never entirely comfortable with training their female students for jobs in the public sphere. In one report, Miss Louisa Imhoff, the superintendent of the industrial department in the Tokyo school, which was now called Aoyama Jo Gakkō, reported with some relief that in 1886 "four [students] have entered the matrimonial state, thus proving that the young ladies of the Industrial Department are in demand as helpmeets" (MEC, Minutes of the Woman's Conference, 1896, 62). Such attitudes were continuously evidenced in the enthusiastic reports of missionary educators about the marriages of their students.

These missionary educators were willing to adapt to almost any new demand upon their school curricula as long as they did not perceive that it would interfere with their object of making Christian wives and mothers. If it would make their graduates more attractive as marriage partners, mission schools were quite willing to teach their students Japanese etiquette, industrial skills, and language, as long as they were able to include a Christian focus alongside these subjects. The principal of the WFMS Yokohama school made this explicitly clear when she wrote to *The Heathen Woman's*

Friend that "[o]ur object is not to teach arithmetic, reading, writing . . . or even to educate. Our object is to make Christians, and our schools are only a means to an end" (WFMS, *HWF,* 1890, 21, no. 4:78–79).

The willingness to adapt to Japanese norms in their attempts to marry off their Christian students sometimes led to a surprising level of acceptance of Japanese customs among some missionaries. WFMS missionary Elizabeth Bender, for example, embraced arranged marriages in a conference paper titled "After Boarding Schools, What—For the Japanese Girl?" Beginning by emphasizing the importance of creating Christian wives and mothers, Bender stated, "I do not hesitate to say that for our girls, after boarding-schools, the Christian home should be the object in view. . . . It is a disappointment to know that in some of our schools, perhaps more or less in all, there is a tendency in the girls to turn away from marriage and domestic life." Following this unsurprising statement, Bender suddenly veered from the ordinary missionary ideals of Western-style marriage and domesticity to advocate the Japanese practice of matchmaking, stating, "Undesirable as the work may be from our American standpoint, we must supplement this teaching by the active work of finding suitable husbands for our girls." Quoting one Christian Japanese matchmaker's assertion that arranging Christian marriages "is one of the surest and quickest ways of evangelizing [Japan]," Bender concluded that "it becomes important for us to control, as far as may be, the marriage of our girls . . . this duty becomes one in which we ought not to fail, however we may shrink from the grave responsibilities involved in it" (MEC, Minutes of the Woman's Conference, 1899, 83–84).

By contrast, Russell and a number of other WFMS missionaries working with her in southern Japan *preferred* their students to remain unmarried in order to carry out their work in the public sphere. Russell resisted the gender ideologies of both her own mission society and of mainstream Japan, refusing the educational agenda of the Woman's Conference and refusing to adapt wholesale to official Japanese programs for women's education. Rather than trying to make Christian mothers, Russell urgently stated that "[i]t is our great object to make Christian workers, efficient workers, to make successors." Thus, Russell aggressively employed graduates of Kwassui in its various departments. Responding to criticisms from other missionaries that her agenda seemed to be more focused on higher education than on the development of truly Christian women, Russell responded that rigorous education was a means for developing Christian sensibilities, even for women. Evoking the liberal theology of the late nineteenth century, Russell proclaimed, "Knowing science is knowing something that will help us know the Creator of science, knowing Music, is knowing how to express thought in sound, knowing art is knowing how to embody thought by means of pencil, brush, or chisel" (MEC, Minutes of the Woman's Conference, 1891, 61).

Unlike many missionaries in the northern islands of Japan, WFMS missionaries in Kyushu, whether in Nagasaki or Fukuoka, even seemed distressed at times over the marriages of their students. WFMS missionary Leonora Seeds, a teacher at Fukuoka Jo Gakkō—which had branched off from Kwassui—stated that "[a] girl surprised us one day by asking if she could get married. Remembering that we must be loyal to the W.F.M.S. and calling to mind a few discourses heard upon the subject of matrimony, we hesitated in giving our consent. However, upon learning that the girl's family had become destitute," Seeds continued, "our hearts melted and within a week she was married to a preacher of the Dutch Reform Mission" (MEC, Minutes of the Woman's Conference, 1892, 81). Since WFMS missionaries in northern Japan seemed quite pleased at the marriage of their students—especially when they married Christian men—it is certainly interesting that Seeds seemed to believe that the WFMS *opposed* the marriages of mission school students. Perhaps Seeds, cut off as she was from the rest of the WFMS since she was living in Kyushu, identified loyalty to the society as being synonymous with loyalty to Elizabeth Russell. Indeed, Russell had come to be known, in the words of her successor Mariana Young, as "the Bishop of Kyushu, because all classes came to her for counsel";[7] and Russell showed much evidence of being disenchanted with marriage. For example, in one report, Russell immediately followed the statement "Death took two of our girls" with the comment that "[a] thief called matrimony also entered our ranks and carried off three of our faithful teachers" (MEC, Japan Mission, *TFJ*, 1903, 6, no. 5:13).

7. Even the general Methodist Episcopal periodical, *Tidings from Japan*, stated that Russell worked in "the Arch-bishop capacity" MEC, Japan Mission, *TFJ*, 1905, 8, no. 1:14–15).

Having experienced the 1890 drop in enrollment, Kwassui staff and faculty worked swiftly to counteract the rising antagonism the school experienced during the year after the Meiji Constitution was promulgated. During the 1890–91 school year, the departments organized events in which Kwassui teachers and students could display to the larger Nagasaki community their talents in music, art, and handiwork. Building on the continued popularity of music studies at Kwassui, Miss Bing's music department offered a new "course of study . . . revised in conformity with the best conservatories in America," and recitals were often held for the public. Miss Imhoff's industrial department "showed off various articles of dress, both Japanese and English, and many specimens of fancy work" (WFMS, Annual Report, 1891, 52). This exhibition—which included displays of "Japanese underwear, kimono, haori, dresses and underwear in foreign style, besides stockings, caps, laces"—demonstrated that the students had been trained in marketable industrial skills. Imhoff's classes became so popular that they began to be attended by both men and women. Similarly, Miss Simmons's new art department exhibited at the closing exercises of the school year "200 drawings from models and from nature, with numerous specimens of wood carving"—including "writing desks, bookracks, and boxes."

Kwassui also countered the perceived antiforeign environment of the early 1890s with its more academically oriented departments. Rather than developing its curriculum to mimic Japanese public schools for girls, as other WFMS schools did, Kwassui further emphasized the elements of its curriculum that set it apart. For example, while other WFMS boarding schools were reducing their English-language programs to more closely resemble public schools, Kwassui brought in a new WFMS missionary, Miss Allen, to head the English department. Another specialist was brought in to head the science department after Emma Everding's death in 1892, and a Japanese teacher was hired in the mathematics department (MEC, Minutes of the Woman's Conference, 1891, 61).

Russell herself headed the Mental and Moral Science Department, which expanded its focus beyond biblical and Christian studies. Her goal was to develop students' critical thinking; she stated, "We often tell the girls that we want to bring them up to a plane of thinking and planning and judging where it will be possible for them to go on and surpass their teachers; indeed it is my belief that if we fail in making successors we *fail* utterly" (MEC, Minutes of the Woman's Conference, 1891, 61). Revealing a focus on a well-rounded education, Russell's personal library included books on moral philosophy, psychology, archaeology, sociology, philology, economics, physiology, chemistry, geology, law, world history, world politics, classic Western literature, Latin, art, and music, as well as theology, biblical studies and hermeneutics.[8]

This revamping and open advertising of the school did indeed appear to attract a renewed interest among Japanese in Nagasaki. Miss Bing, for example, stated that the music department "doubled in its numbers." By the time of her 1891 report to the WFMS, Russell was optimistic enough, despite the low enrollment of the previous school year, to state that the "reaction against foreign influence . . . is passing, and the new year opens with increased enrollment and renewed interest in departments of work" (WFMS, Annual Report, 1891, 51).

The Educational Ordinances of 1899

Having watched her risks pay off during the last two decades of the nineteenth century, on the eve of the political transformations of 1899, when the revised treaties would go into effect, Russell expressed confidence that mission schools would survive. Aware of the possibility of government intervention in mission schools, Russell nevertheless argued that not much would change after the Japanese government gained more power over foreigners in Japan, for "[b]y the new treaties all manner of business is invited. While our schools are means to the end of establishing a broad Christianity in Japan, each school is a business house. The Japanese Government will not think of interfering with the internal management of schools any more than it will with the internal management of the Hong Kong and Shanghai Bank, or other commercial institutions" (MEC, Japan Mission, *TFJ*, 1898, 1, no. 11:9). Other missionaries were less optimistic that there

8. Russell's personal library is preserved in the Russell Collection at Kwassui Gakuin in Nagasaki.

would be a smooth transition; as one WFMS missionary stated, "[f]or five years both the foreign and Japanese population of Japan have been in a state of disquietude, now expectant, now anxious, over the results of the treaty revision. . . . Even the missionaries, with their rich inheritance of faith and hope, have shared to a certain extent in the general uneasiness. . . . Thus far their schools have been entirely under their own control; but now they will become subject to Japanese inspection and Japanese school regulations" (MEC, Minutes of the Woman's Conference, 1899, 11–12).

Despite Russell's confidence, in 1899 the government did put new pressures on mission schools. Like all mission schools in Japan, the WFMS schools were compelled to seriously reevaluate their mission and educational strategies after 1899, as they came under Japanese law. Even the most pessimistic missionaries were shocked when, less than a month after they came under Japanese jurisdiction, the government passed Ordinance Number 12 banning religious instruction in primary schools and in government-recognized middle and high schools. These laws were clearly an attack on Christian schools. The most immediate effect of the ordinance was the removal of primary-level students from the mission schools, as it unequivocally stated that they were not to have religious instruction in any school. Unwilling to give up their existing Christian curriculum and unsure of how to proceed strategically, the mission schools initially found nothing else to do than to surrender their primary-level students. The year following the ordinance, for example, Kwassui lost forty students (*Kwassui Jo Gakko. 1879 1939*, 9).

Moreover, mission schools' programs of higher education were now put in a position where they had "very serious disabilities." For example, the Congregationalists' Kobe College, the first female mission school to receive recognition by the government under the new laws, was designated by the government as a "miscellaneous school" rather than as a school of higher education, since the school's missionaries desired to continue religious instruction. As Noriko Kawamura Ishii states, since graduates of a miscellaneous school were not qualified to apply to the Tokyo Women's Normal School, one of the only teacher-training institutions for Japanese women, this was a significant "sacrifice . . . to protect Christian education" (2004, 130).

In addition to Ordinance Number 12, female mission schools were further challenged in 1899 by the Act of Women's High Schools and Vocational Schools. This act required all prefectures to establish four-year high schools for women. While in the mid-1890s there were only seven public higher schools for women, there were forty-five such schools by 1900, and eighty-nine by 1905 (Marshall 1994, 74). Additionally, by 1900 the government was able to waive tuition fees for public schools providing compulsory education, which, not surprisingly, resulted in a large boost in enrollment; in particular, the number of girls entering public school soared (72). Mission schools for girls and women no longer had the edge, as they soon were competing with free public schools and an unprecedented number of female higher schools. Thus, not only did they have more and better public schools to compete with, but mission schools were often hampered by foregoing official status as a higher school in order to continue teaching religion in their curriculum.

In January 1900, Christian educators in Japan held an Educational Convention to discuss how to respond to the government regulations. Missionaries expressed their outrage at the meeting, balking at having their religious activities regulated by the Japanese government in any way. Reflecting their displeasure, they wrote a resolution criticizing the Japanese government:

> The Constitution of the Empire grants religious liberty; the Instruction of the Educational Department definitely and more completely than ever forbids all teaching of religion, as well as religious exercises, to all schools having government recognition. We feel that this position of the Educational Department is contrary to the spirit of the Constitution of the Empire, in practically restricting the liberty of parents in deciding upon the education of their children. We do not here raise any objections to the Educational Department making such restrictions for *public* schools supported by *public* funds; but we feel that to put these same limitations upon *private* schools supported by *private* funds works great injustice. (*Japan Evangelist* 1900, 7, no. 2:56)

Other than registering their displeasure, however, missionaries realized that they could not change the new educational ordinances. The plan of action that became the most popular among missionaries was to develop their own system of universities, colleges, and normal schools to compete with Japanese educational institutions, so that graduates of mission middle and higher schools would have opportunities paralleling those of the graduates of government-approved secondary schools. At the Educational Convention it was agreed that in order to continue to attract students to mission schools there needed to be a Christian Japanese University "of the highest order. . . . with buildings and appliances of the best kind, and with endowments, fellowships, and scholarships that would be sufficient not only for ordinary work but for sending its most promising teachers and pupils to the seats of learning in the West and giving them the best opportunities that can be had in their particular lines of study."

While these missionary leaders were particularly concerned about education for boys and men in their plan, their call for increasing the quality of higher education in mission schools was influential among leaders of female mission schools as well. While up to this point a number of female mission schools had been less rigorous in their academic training than in religious instruction (despite the calls for higher education among more progressive missionary women), they now felt the pressure to raise their academic standards or perish. A leader of the Educational Convention, William Imbrie, revealed the desperate situation of missionaries when he stated that it was crucial for them to take "pains to make it increasingly clear" that mission schools did *not* "exist solely for the sake of the propagation of Christianity." He called on all missionary educators to "see that the general education that we give is as good as we can make it" (*Japan Evangelist* 1900, 7, no. 2:42). Many missionaries were realizing, as more progressive missionaries like Russell always had, that if female mission schools offered a superior education to that of the government schools, they could attract women desiring a more academically rigorous education.

Given this heightened emphasis on raising the standards of mission schools, it is not surprising that *The Japan Evangelist* issue following the special edition on the Educational Convention featured Kwassui Jo Gakkō as an example of a successful female mission school. Stating that Kwassui had already developed a collegiate department in 1889, *The Japan Evangelist* called for an endowment for Kwassui to develop its program of training teachers. The article ended by emphasizing that since "[m]ission work is becoming more and more a problem . . . [it] is the part of wisdom to double our endeavor in training our students and all other Christians to help themselves. To this end we plead for endowment for 'Kwassui,' not to educate the multitude, but to train the few who may become the representative women, leaders among their own people" (*Japan Evangelist* 1900, 7, no. 3:78).

In 1900 Augusta Dickerson, the principal of the WFMS school in Hakodate, revealed the new willingness among many WFMS missionaries to finally follow Kwassui's lead. In a paper titled "A Unified System for Our Schools," presented to the Woman's Conference in 1900, Dickerson urged WFMS missionaries to update their pedagogies for girls' and women's education. She stated, "The world moves. It moves forward in educational methods as in other things, and we shall not be imprisoned with Galileo for believing it. . . . The very highest and the most perfect university is not too high nor too good for our young Japanese sisters. Christian Education is the noble handmaiden who shall lead the women of this land to the full possession of their birthright,—the inheritance of the knowledge of the ages."

Like female missionary societies around Japan, the WFMS began to focus on developing their own normal schools, which would help deflect any disadvantage mission school graduates might find in attempting to enter government normal schools. Reflecting this shift in strategy, Dickerson stated, "Our great need is for trained teachers . . . who are to be our successors. . . . Let us plan so broadly and wisely that our education will not seem a mere ornament, but a necessary agent in the development of God-given facilities" (MEC, Minutes of the Woman's Conference, 1900, 83–85).

The ultimate effect of the government educational ordinances on mission schools for girls and women, then, was to push them to advance their curriculum to a level beyond what many WFMS missionaries had originally envisioned. For example, Aoyama Jogakuin, the WFMS school founded by Dora Schoonmaker, developed a higher-education program by 1900 and became a very well-respected women's college in Japan. Focusing on higher education proved successful, as WFMS boarding schools continued to report full and growing enrollments into the 1900s.

Even though the educational ordinances of 1899 did not turn out to be as devastating for their schools as missionaries feared, they had the effect of putting missionaries "in their place" by making clear that the Japanese, not Westerners, were in charge of the future of the country. The ordinances forced missionaries to acknowledge that they had no choice but to market their schools to fit Japanese interests, or fail utterly in their endeavors.

6

"One World-wide Sisterhood"

Advocating a Conditional Equality

> She is our sister, who doth wear
> The robe of womanhood. . . .
> One world-wide sisterhood declare
> Beneath the Pine and Palm.
>
> —Mary E. Dustin, "Who Is Our Sister?" 1873

As their relationships with Japanese evolved over the years, missionary women ultimately became a voice for liberal ideals of ethnic and gender equality back in the United States. Bonded with the people with whom they lived and worked, and admiring the country's development into a powerful nation-state, by the early-twentieth-century missionaries had gained a new level of respect for Japan, and they worked to change Americans' condescending attitudes and discriminatory practices toward Japanese, including Japanese living in the United States. American proponents of immigrant exclusion policies—which in the early twentieth century included a strong focus on excluding Japanese immigration—even targeted missionaries as one of their prime adversaries. Through their publications, missionaries sought to teach their denominational supporters in the United States how to think and talk in more sensitive ways about ethnicities and cultures other than their own.

Moreover, over time many women involved in the Woman's Foreign Missionary Society of the Methodist Episcopal Church came to believe that the Christianity they were promoting was not only about uplifting women in non-Christian contexts but also was about promoting women's rights back in the United States. In widely dispersed treatises by leaders of the women's mission movement, women's spiritual, social, and political emancipation was presented as part and parcel of the "true Christianity" advocated by missionaries. While they still believed Christianity was the salvation of the world, missionary women came into the twentieth century with a Christian vision reshaped by international experiences, and a revised understanding of women's "world-wide sisterhood."

The literature of the WFMS, from its inception in 1869 through World War I and its aftermath, reveals a complicated, evolving interconnection between ideologies of ethnicity, imperialism, and gender in Protestant women's thought. The primary purpose of WFMS literature was first and foremost to raise money to support missionary enterprises overseas and thus in many ways catered to the tastes and emotions of its reading audience to solicit their subscriptions and generous contributions to the cause. As it also served as a venue for missionaries to share their experiences overseas, however, it simultaneously contained material that would challenge readers to move beyond their received assumptions about women's work and foreign lands, as missionaries articulated a vision for women of the twentieth century to transcend boundaries of nation and gender.

Elizabeth and May Russell

Like numerous other WFMS missionaries throughout the world, Elizabeth Russell represented a vision of progressive womanhood, a vision that included respectful, even intimate, relationships with people of varied cultures and ethnicities. Elizabeth's admiration for Japan's political and economic successes was coupled with her love for Japanese people at a more personal level. Most importantly, her adoption of a Japanese infant in 1885, whom she named Ellen May Russell, profoundly shaped her perspectives on the Japanese "race." Elizabeth literally came to see Japanese as her kin as she raised May with her Kwassui family, and she was angered by the discrimination her daughter and other Japanese faced when they entered U.S. national boundaries. Although Elizabeth was slow to become cognizant of her own ethnocentrism, through raising May she experienced the reality of racial discrimination as a personal wound. By the 1900s, after years of having May and the faculty and students at Kwassui as family, Elizabeth spoke of the Japanese in general as her own flesh and blood.

During her first years in Japan, before adopting May, Elizabeth was prone to making condescending remarks about Japanese (and other nonwhite people). In 1883, for example, Elizabeth wrote to Emma Tolbert, a longtime friend in the United States, "Your efforts with your young American of African descent is not unlike some of our efforts with the Japanese, in many respects the Japanese remind me of the freedmen. They have the same indifference to the future. They will have a good time today to be sure they have nothing for tomorrow. . . . But when they do get an idea of making money they become very greedy and cheat in every possible way to increase their honest earnings, they get such an idea of earning money without working for it."

Years later, after raising May, Elizabeth would find such racist overgeneralizations offensive. Elizabeth, who had not expected to become a mother at age forty-eight, was delighted with her Japanese daughter, expressing her joy in her letters to Emma. "Did I tell you about my baby?" she wrote, "She is a real sweet little thing—a great comfort to us all, the other ladies love her as much as I do." Apparently, according to Elizabeth's account, the baby came to her after a relative of a former student, facing a divorce, felt compelled to give up the infant, and the former student suggested giving the baby to the principal of Kwassui. When the baby was only a few days old, a family member brought her to Kwassui, and Elizabeth agreed to take in the infant at the encouragement of her co-workers. Having served as a second mother to her sister Julia's children before leaving for Japan in 1879, Elizabeth found that the new child in her life helped ease the pain of separation from her beloved nieces and nephews. In 1889, when May was four, Elizabeth wrote to Emma, "My sister's boys were in dresses when I went away. Now they are almost young men. The babies are all gone. My Japanese baby is all the baby we have now."

Elizabeth's journey toward a respectful relationship with the Japanese, including her own daughter, was complicated; like other American missionaries, her thinking about ethnicity did not evolve quickly or smoothly.

Elizabeth approached May's upbringing, at least initially, in the way missionaries first approached their work in Japan: She dressed May up as an American girl, all the while highly aware of her nonwhite features, just as in the early years missionaries desired to clothe Japan in the garments of American culture while seeing the Japanese, to varying degrees, as "other." "I send you her photo," Elizabeth wrote to Emma, "I dress her American fashion—but anyone could tell from her raven hair & eyes that she was a Jap." Calling May a Jap was not a direct racial slur in Elizabeth's circle but rather a diminutive, "cutesy" name for Japanese people; while perhaps it reflected a feeling of condescension toward Japanese that Elizabeth had at the time, she did not intend the word to have the hateful connotations that it was starting to take on in some contexts. Elizabeth was most familiar with the way the term was used in the foreign mission movement; missionary literature for children during this era, for example, included a book called *Jack and the Japs,* and another children's mission book titled *Good Times in Japan* was advertised as having "a picture of five little Japs gaily floating out to sea with inverted umbrellas as most satisfactory craft" (WFMS, *WMF,* 1905, 37, no. 2:47). White Americans involved in the mission movement in the late nineteenth and early twentieth centuries seemed oblivious at times to the growing anti-Japanese movement in the United States—especially in California—in which the word "Jap" was a commonly used racial slur (Takaki 1998, 180–82). However, as discussed later in this chapter, over time missionaries did become more cognizant of anti-Japanese prejudice in the United States, causing them to scrutinize their own language more carefully.

Rather than raising May in the private setting of the home, Elizabeth raised her in the communal setting created by the faculty and boarding students at Kwassui, which enabled her to continue working as a teacher and the principal of the school. Elizabeth wrote, "That baby was the queen of the household and school." Despite this claim, however, Elizabeth did not indulge May in much pampering. Elizabeth continued to be fully focused on her career, even with a baby at her side, and May was like a young apprentice from the earliest age. Elizabeth wrote in her journal, "When Baby May came to be one or two years old she wanted to be by me all the time. . . . As I sat at my desk writing, she wanted to be by me. So I bought her a high chair and set her on it and divided the desk by laying a rule and calling it a fence and made the rule that Baby must stay on baby's side of the fence and Mama must stay on Mama's side of the fence and she never trespassed. This rule was always observed and thus avoided all trouble between us."

When May was eleven years old, in 1896, Elizabeth sent her to the United States to live with Julia, and thus Elizabeth's sister effectively raised May from age eleven until adulthood. Julia had been a widow since her husband, George Ephraim Chapman, had died in 1882. Upon Ephraim's death, Julia (pregnant at the time) and her children had moved in with her father, John Russell, who was living alone in Berlin, Pennsylvania, having outlived three wives. In 1890, John Russell died while Elizabeth was on furlough in the United States with May, and during this furlough Elizabeth had helped Julia relocate to Delaware, Ohio, the home of Ohio Wesleyan University, so that Julia's children could have access to a good university education while staying near their mother. Now Elizabeth wanted the same educational opportunity for May. Elizabeth wrote in her journal, "On October 3, 1896 Miss Leonora Seeds sailed for home and I sent my baby May with her. I wanted her well trained to teach English in our Kwassui. It was hard to part with her." Elizabeth kept in close contact with May, but she rarely had the opportunity to visit her for the next fourteen years, as May spent ten years in the American school system before entering into the four-year college program at Ohio Wesleyan. Elizabeth wrote wistfully in her journal: "In June, 1906 — How I should have liked to have been in Delaware, Ohio that month. My darling graduated from High School." Elizabeth was thrilled to be able to take a furlough as May finished college, and she attended May's graduation from Ohio Wesleyan in 1910. "Yes, she really graduated," Elizabeth exclaimed in a letter to Emma. "It seemed so strange—seemed but a little while ago since she came to me—an infant, and now a woman grown and done with college."

Her devotion to May helped to develop Elizabeth's critical awareness of the racism nonwhites faced in the United States. In a letter to Emma soon after May's college graduation, she wrote that she was anxious for May to return with her to Japan and teach at Kwassui because "racial prejudice is so strong [in the United States] that she could not get a Situation."

Upon their return to Japan, May did well as teacher at Kwassui, and Elizabeth wrote proudly, "[May] is a lovely girl, sweet in disposition, thorough going in her work, and is friendly & has friends alike among Japanese & Americans." Elizabeth had managed to make Kwassui Jo Gakkō a haven for women who, like her own daughter, had multicultural identities. An early-twentieth-century report from Kwassui Jo Gakkō revealed that girls and women with various national and ethnic identities attended the school, including students who were "Russian, Jew[ish], English, American, Chinese, Eurasian, Japanese, [and] Loo Chooan" (MEC, Japan Mission, *TFJ,* 1901, 4, no. 12:11).[1]

Elizabeth Russell's description of the thirty-fifth anniversary of Kwassui, in 1915, illuminated the extent to which she had transcended her ethnocentrism after three and a half decades in Japan, as she spoke of the school's multicultural alumna not as "other" than herself, but like long-lost family; the event revealed how far everyone had come in their understanding of difference. Elizabeth wrote that

> it was a delightful week . . . [for] me to see so many of the old graduates come back. . . . Think of it girls working yet who graduated 27 years ago. . . . It was a week of rejuvenation for them to be here & see each other, [coming] from different parts of the country as teachers & Bible women . . . how jubilant they were . . . & I was as much a child as any of them. One night they gathered in a room & talked & talked until near midnight, the old times over. A very funny incident occurred at the banquet, one of the old girls in responding to a toast, said among other things that I was the first person she had ever seen with blue eyes & she could not understand how I could see with blue eyes, of course it brought the house down.

Elizabeth came to truly love Japanese women, and May was one of the chief joys of her life. When Elizabeth retired at age eighty-two in 1919, May, whose health was failing with "incipient Tuberculosis," returned with her to Delaware, Ohio. They moved in with Julia, who by that point was a virtual invalid and would rapidly deteriorate until her death in 1922.

1. "Loo Choo" is a reference to the Ryukyu Islands, which include Okinawa.

Elizabeth—distraught at the condition in which she found her ailing sister, and having trouble adjusting to "this American way of living" and "this dull town"—clung to May as never before. Elizabeth spent almost all of her retirement money sending May to nearby sanitariums, stating that she "would give anything [for May] to be rid of that dreadful disease." While they had spent years apart in the past, during these twilight years Elizabeth could hardly bear to be parted from May for any length of time. Once, during a healthy spell, May went to visit some friends in Iowa, and Elizabeth wrote to Emma Tolbert, "I miss her so much, she will be gone 10 days or two weeks." Despite all their efforts at fighting the disease, May died in a tuberculosis sanitarium in 1924 at age thirty-nine. May's tragically young death must have been a crushing blow to Elizabeth, who was left to live the last four years of her life without her beloved daughter. When Elizabeth died on September 6, 1928, the Kwassui alumnae purchased a large tombstone for her grave in Ohio, engraved with a phrase Elizabeth had used to express her love for those who had been everything to her in life: "If you could see it, you would find the girlhood of Japan written upon my heart."

May, for her part, did not leave many records of her life behind. Her perspectives on her childhood, her mother, and her place in the world are lost, save the tantalizing Shakespearean quote she chose to go with her college yearbook picture: "Though I am not splenetive and rash,/Yet have I something in me, dangerous." May, and others like her, were continually challenging white Americans to reexamine their prejudices.

Representing the "Other" in Missionary Literature

Missionaries had always seen themselves as the friends of nonwhite, non-Christian populations, even in the days when they looked upon them as heathens. Like Elizabeth Russell, as missionaries struggled to be true friends to their nonwhite neighbors, colleagues, and family in their host countries, they revised their thinking and language about the "other." From the earliest days of the American mission movement, missionaries believed themselves to be exceptionally progressive, as they were criticized and mocked by advocates of white supremacist ideologies. In the early nineteenth century, the polygenist theory that different races were in fact different species was gaining ground among leading scientists (Gossett 1997), and proponents of this theory believed missionaries were misguided in thinking that any fundamental change could be brought about among nonwhite populations around the world. In 1848, Josiah C. Nott, a major contributor to the polygenist school, stated, "All the historical records of the past tell us of the same moral and physical differences of races which exist at the present day, and we can only judge the future by the past. The numberless attempts by the Caucasian race, during several thousand years, to bring the Mongol, Malay, Indian and Negro under the same religion, laws, manners, customs, etc., have failed, and must continue to fail" (Nott [1849] 1969, 17; qtd. in Schueller 1998, 38–39).

This theory was generally opposed by evangelical Protestants in the United States because it challenged the Genesis story of a single creation of humanity. As a result, polygenesists dismissed proponents of the monogenist theory—that all humans were of a single species—as being deluded by religious superstition. Charles Darwin's *On the Origin of Species,* published in 1859, discredited the polygenist theory, but sparked a new theory supporting racism—that the different races reflected a single human species at different stages of evolution, an idea that was often perpetuated by Social Darwinists. While notions of racial hierarchy did find their way into mission rhetoric, most missionaries tended to find both the polygenist theory and the most racist forms of Social Darwinism to be threats to their cause; to deny the redeemability of any human race was to deny the power of Christ.

Mission literature was filled with stories of the potential of "heathens" to be transformed from barbarians to virtuous citizens, as understood by Western elites. As one late-nineteenth-century missionary proclaimed, displaying a classic example of liberal racism: "The first thing Christianity does for [heathens] is the same that Jesus did for the blind man. It says, 'Go, wash.' The next thing, naturally, is the same that came to the demoniac: he was found 'clothed.' I trust that all else may follow; that whereas they have been blind, they may see, and be in their right minds" (WFMS, *HWF,* 1874, 5, no. 10:637). Discounting notions of inherent differences among the races, in 1875 a missionary wife wrote, "I have often been questioned in regard to the characteristics and capabilities of the women of India, and have endeavored, in a book that is now going through the press, . . . to show that Hindostanee women possess powers of mind equal to those of the women of Christian lands, and that they only need the inspiration of Christianity to raise them to an equality with ourselves" (WFMS, *HWF*, 1875, 6, no. 10:839).

In the early years of the mission movement, evangelical Protestants believed that the perceived degradation of foreign cultures was caused by false religion, not by inherent racial characteristics. Thus, through conversion all races could achieve the heights of human civilization, which missionaries unquestioningly associated with Western culture.

The approach of contrasting dirty, unclothed, crazed heathens with Christian converts, however, was increasingly problematized as the missionary movement evolved; some missionaries grew uncomfortable with the way this continued to promote racist stereotypes about non-Western cultures. It was always a struggle among more progressively minded individuals in the mission movement to convey the "other" with a sense of respect and to convince their fellow missionaries and denominational supporters to view those they sought to uplift as equals. India missionary Rev. James Thoburn—the brother of the WFMS's celebrated first missionary, Isabella Thoburn—wrote an article in an 1871 issue of *The Heathen Woman's Friend* urging more care in describing non-Christian peoples, stating:

> Horrible stories are sometimes told about the heathen, which are true, without being truthful. . . . The facts related have actually occurred, but the manner of telling them does not give a truthful picture of heathen society. I most earnestly recommend all true friends of missions to be very sparing of sensational stories about murdered and mangled children, brutal parents, loathsome sin and crime, and all the long catalogue of horrible things which some people think necessary for spice to a missionary meeting. (WFMS, *HWF*, 1871, 3, no. 5:199)

Despite Reverend Thoburn's plea, in the very next issue the author of the "Children's Corner" exclaimed: "Why, [pagans in India] just kill off hundreds and hundreds of [girls] when they are little bits of babies. Not such a bad thing for the children, to be sure, for they will go straight to Heaven; and if they live to grow big, they will never be sent to school . . . or be treated as if they were anybody. It is dreadfully wicked of their fathers and mothers to kill them, though" (WFMS, *HWF,* 1871, 3, no.6:218). As Kwok Pui-lan and other scholars have pointed out, such images of non-Western cultures contributed heavily to long-term Western perceptions of colonized peoples as the "other," in *need* of the imperialist takeover of the civilizing West. Kwok states: "Missionary religious journals, memoirs, and travel writings, reaching to grassroots women sitting in the pews, were important sources of information about Third World women at the turn of the nineteenth century. The condescending attitude toward women of other parts of the world and the missionary impulse to save them remains deeply lodged in Western women's minds even to the present" (2002, 67).

While the sensational and demeaning stories about foreign cultures continued to be sprinkled throughout the pages of mission literature, however, as some missionaries grew to respect their host cultures, their evolving perspectives were also disseminated through mission magazines. Americans involved in missions during this era of high imperialism were not monolithic in their discourses on gender and race, and the pages of *The Heathen Woman's Friend* (renamed *Woman's Missionary Friend* in 1896) reflected this. The magazine highlighted multiple perspectives as it printed articles by U.S.-based women who operated the quickly growing organization, by missionaries in the field, and by non-Western women who worked with missionaries, in addition to a range of articles by others sympathetic to women's missions.

Missionaries sent many positive portrayals of non-Western cultures to mission magazines and demystified the exotic, to some degree, for Americans (while also fueling their romantic imaginings about places far away). The pages of *The Heathen Woman's Friend* and *Woman's Missionary Friend* contained stories of "ordinary" American women traveling and living perfectly well in a myriad of cultures around the world. The magazines were filled with articles by missionary women with titles such as "A Walk By the Yangtse"; "Good Times in Rangoon"; "Beautiful Malaysia"; "Making Calls in Africa"; "Bridal Festivities in Burma"; "Christmas in the Philippines"; "A Country Trip in Korea"; and "Java, 'The Pearl of the East.'" Since the

WFMS was hampered by the men's General Mission Board from publicly speaking about their mission work at Methodist gatherings, it was essential for the organization to utilize literature and personal correspondence from missionaries to give American Protestant women a sense of connection with women around the world. The missionaries' "detailed information of the work under their care" made the distant lands in which they toiled seem real to their supporters. One missionary described how she had ignited the imagination of a supporter back in the United States when she had sent her "a bit of fern, from Lal Bagh, in Lucknow"; the woman wrote to the missionary: "The little leaf you sent whispered to me of our girls in India. A trifle, to be sure; yet nothing ever brought them so near my heart" (WFMS, *HWF,* 1873, 5, no. 4:541).

Even with its many limitations, missionary literature was the first to provide the average American Protestant woman with a conditional knowledge about countries around the world. Describing life in China, for example, in an 1874 article in *The Heathen Woman's Friend,* a missionary incidentally introduced many readers to feng shui, most likely for the first time, when she wrote, "Foochow boasts a telegraph at last. . . . Several years ago foreign residents decided to erect a short line at their own expense, and proceeded to put up the poles, which the natives pulled down at once, because they injured the *fung-shui*—'wind and water.' A proclamation is now attached to each pole forbidding interference" (WFMS, *HWF,* 1874, 6, no. 4:735).

In addition to the information provided in their monthly magazine, leaders of the WFMS encouraged local branches of their organization to create study groups to learn more in depth about the countries in which their missionaries labored, using the textbooks of the interdenominational Central Committee on the United Study of Foreign Missions (CCUSFM). Supported by seven major American Protestant denominations, including the Methodist Episcopal Church, the CCUSFM published textbooks annually from 1901 to 1938 and sold hundreds of thousands of copies. As Nancy A. Hardesty recounts in her article "The Scientific Study of Missions" (2003), in the first decade of the twentieth century, the CCUSFM published detailed books about India, China, Japan, the African continent, the islands of the Pacific, the Near East, and Latin America, complete with accompanying study guides, posters, and maps. According to one story, at a dinner party in Washington, D.C., a woman so impressed a foreign diplomat with her extensive knowledge of cultures around the world that he assumed her husband was also a diplomat; instead, to his surprise, she informed him that she had gained her knowledge from studying "the textbooks of the Central Committee on the United Study of Foreign Missions" (Hardesty 2003, 106).

By the end of the nineteenth century, many of the leaders of the American mission movement sought to portray non-Western cultures with a language that well-intentioned, liberal-minded Americans considered respectful. For example, in the 1890s, WFMS missionaries in Japan pushed their U.S.-based headquarters to stop using the word *heathen.* In October of 1895, the General Executive Committee of the Woman's Foreign Missionary Society held a debate over whether to change the name of their organization's central monthly publication, *The Heathen Woman's Friend,* largely because of pressure from missionaries in Japan. The request that the Publication Committee "consider a change of name by which the term 'heathen' shall be eliminated" was met with some resistance; those opposed to the motion stated that they would "earnestly request the General Executive Committee to leave us the name that expresses so much." Nevertheless, a motion was raised to make the change because "Missionaries and other friends of our Society have objected to the name of our paper the *Heathen Woman's Friend,* as being a misnomer, and have found it a hindrance to their work, and in their efforts to increase its circulation" (WFMS, *HWF,* 1895, 27, no. 6:161).

Numerous missionaries were called upon to give their opinion on whether "the word 'heathen' was especially objectionable," and the minutes noted that missionaries working in Japan and India, in particular, did indeed find the word problematic (WFMS, *HWF,* 1895, 27, no. 6:162). After a close vote of fifteen in favor and fourteen opposed, the word *heathen* was struck from the publication title, and the new title, *Woman's Missionary Friend,* was adopted.[2]

2. The first issue to carry the title *Woman's Missionary Friend* was published in January 1896 (vol. 27, no. 7).

It is no surprise that Japanese or anyone else who came into contact with the English-speaking world took offense when the word was applied to them; if they were to look up the word in any standard English-language dictionary of the day, they would see that one of its prominent definitions was "an uncivilized man; a barbarian." Yet it was not easy to convince supporters of the missionary cause to give up the word, and it continued to be used in articles contributed to the *Woman's Missionary Friend* and in other missionary literature for years after the General Executive Committee of the WFMS had rejected the publication's initial title. For many missionary-minded Americans, the word's other meaning, defined in the 1868 version of Webster's *American Dictionary of the English Language* as "an individual of the pagan or unbelieving nations, or those which worship idols and do not acknowledge the true God; a pagan; an idolater; an irreligious, unthinking person," was most fitting for non-Christians. Moreover, the idea that Christianity was at the foundation of civilization—and its inverse, that paganism lay at the foundation of barbarism—was a deeply embedded assumption among many Americans. For women interested in missions, the term "heathen" had also taken on another meaning that touched the pulse of their movement: It evoked the degradation and abuse of women, whom they believed to be the particular benefactors of Christianity and civilization.

It was only when these assumptions began to unravel that the term "heathen" began to fall out of favor, first among missionaries in the field, and then among their supporters back in the United States. The rise of modern Japan, in particular, challenged American Protestants' notions of heathendom, as the country became civilized according to Western standards even as it remained predominantly non-Christian. Helen Barrett Montgomery, an author of six CCUSFM textbooks and numerous other publications, and who had an inestimable influence on Protestant women at this time, was even so bold as to write to her American Protestant audience that to "describe Buddhism as paganism merely shows a lamentable amount of ignorance. After all, any religion must be largely judged by its effects on the lives of its adherents, and judged by that standard I do not think, as regards the Japanese, either Buddhism or Shintoism ought to be sweepingly condemned" (1909, 45).

Such radical ideas were slow to catch on. Ten years after the WFMS missionary magazine changed its name, a contributor to a 1906 issue seems to have only partially caught on to the idea of speaking about non-Westerners with more respectful language; after stating that her group had read in their CCUSFM textbook that "the Japanese do not like to be called heathen . . . so we now think of them as our brothers," she went on to say how the group enjoyed learning about "their queer ways" (WFMS, *WMF,* 1906, 38, no. 1:12). The editors of the *Woman's Missionary Friend* found it necessary to repeatedly point out to mission study groups in the United States that "[s]ympathetic mission study is never helped by making our 'little brown brother' ridiculous. . . . In all discussion emphasize the similarities rather than the differences of character between yourself and them. By this method of approach, manners and customs will not seem 'queer,' for that would be evidence of anything but a cosmopolitan spirit" (WFMS, *WMF,* 1905, 37, no. 2:57).

Despite their slow reception, liberal language and ideas continued to be disseminated through missionary literature as the twentieth century progressed, gradually pervading American Protestant consciousness. Challenging white Anglo-Saxon-Protestant arrogance became a constant theme in the pages of the *Woman's Missionary Friend.* An editorial in an issue from 1907 described to readers how barbaric American wedding customs would seem to a Chinese woman in order to make the point that "it all depends on the point of view"; the piece concluded by stating that "it is just possible that we Americans, with our Anglo-Saxon feeling of superiority to all the world, may still have a few things to learn in matters of taste and tolerance" (WFMS, *WMF,* 1907, 39, no. 6:203). While the editorial conflated "Americans" with "Anglo-Saxons" as if the two were one and the same, the article's well-intentioned purpose was to challenge its largely Anglo-Saxon audience to reconsider their ethnocentricity. Another article conveyed the message of a Chinese man who "told us [missionaries] that we assumed an attitude of superiority that was very antagonistic to our work . . . [he] added that Jesus Christ would surely make no distinction between the Chinese and the European." The missionary author of this piece concluded that this Chinese man "told us many things that were true . . . the coat was surely made to order and I hope we all put it on" (39, 10:363). The author of a piece titled "Christless—Not Heathen" informed *WMF* readers that "German scholars tell us the roots of all European philosophies strike down into the ancient philosophies of India," concluding that "[s]urely, the word 'heathen' is most unscientifically and thoughtlessly applied to the polished Hindu; to the dignified, intelligent Chinese with his pre-historic lineage; to the Japanese with his wealth of poetic symbols both in the arts and letters of his country" (WFMS, *WMF*, 1912, 44, no. 8:279).

While a Social Darwinist notion of racial hierarchy, so pervasive in American thought in the late nineteenth and early twentieth centuries, did make its way into missionary literature—as some contributors indicated that Japanese were farther along an evolutionary chart than other peoples (as one editor of the *Woman's Missionary Friend* stated, missionary work spanned between "darkest Africa and fairest Japan")—missionaries frequently challenged this notion, citing the biblical principle that "all are one in Christ Jesus." In an 1906 article titled "A Plea for the Congo Free State," WFMS missionary Clementina Butler—the daughter of missionaries William and Clementina Butler, who had helped to found the WFMS—called upon American Protestant women to publicize the fight for independence in the Congo, stating, "Why should we in our happy homes trouble ourselves about the sufferings of the black people in the Congo? . . . If God has made 'of one blood all nations to dwell on the earth,' he has also made their nerves of the one material and their hearts to beat with the same joy or sorrow as ours . . . if we have the spirit of Christ, we too must be touched with the sorrows of humanity, of our brothers and sisters, wherever they may be" (WFMS, *WMF*, 1906, 38, no. 2:46–47).

Missionary rhetoric in the early twentieth century generally focused on minimizing cultural difference as a strategy for combating racism among ordinary American Protestants, rather than attempting to convince their audience that difference was acceptable. Despite the limits of this approach in fully challenging white American ethnocentrism, supporters of missions optimistically believed that the movement would make overt forms of racism less and less acceptable among their denominational supporters. The *Woman's Missionary Friend* touted missionaries as having made "invaluable contributions to the world's knowledge of mankind, and [their] sympathetic portrayal helps in the realization of the great ideal of universal brotherhood" (WFMS, *WMF*, 1908, 40, no. 5:154).

Images of Wartime Japan

With this rise of liberal antiracist rhetoric among leaders of the women's missionary movement, the example of Japan seemed to be an ideal way to challenge white American ethnocentricity. By the end of the nineteenth century, Japanese had successfully embraced many of the elements of Western society that Europeans and Euro-Americans had claimed as the hallmarks of white supremacy: a disciplined and victorious modern military; a constitutional government; a public, modern educational system; a booming industrialized economy, complete with a nationwide railway system; and modern standards of public health and hygiene, to name a few. Japan's case did not require ethnocentric Americans to reconsider their standards for measuring progress and civility; it only required that they reconsider their assumptions that the white race alone was capable of achieving the highest forms of civilization. In this vein, Elizabeth Russell wrote, "I consider it one of the greatest privileges of my life that, along with my missionary work, I was in Japan at the time I was and so was enabled to witness the phenomenal development of that interesting people . . . and lo! Now Japan has won a place among the five great powers of the earth—unparalleled history!" ("Pioneer Days" n.d.).

Japan's military victory in the Sino-Japanese War of 1894–95, and even more importantly, its victory over the Western, "Christian" nation of Russia in 1905, revealed in no uncertain terms that Japan was becoming a modern, imperialist nation-state. In an 1896 *Japan Evangelist* article, written at the end of the Sino-Japanese war, an anonymous Japanese wrote: "[T]he people of Europe and America did not expect to find in this part of the earth an active intelligent race, capable of comprehending their ideas. . . . we are afraid that our country was not taken very seriously by foreign people in general. . . . Now all this is changed, or at least is changing, since the successful issue of the war with China raised Japan in the eyes of the world. . . . it seems to be left for Japan to show that the sphere of civilization may be supra-racial" (1896, 3, no. 4:209, 210).

Japan's victories were among the most shattering challenges to Victorian ideologies of social/racial Darwinism that had legitimated *Western* imperialism, including ideas that Caucasians were the pinnacle of human evolution, that Christianity was the pinnacle of religious and cultural evolution, and that both whiteness and Christianity were the necessary ingredients of civilization (understood in terms of technological and political power). Now, a people who were neither white nor predominantly Christian were taking on the trappings of modern civilization—and succeeding so well at it that they were becoming a serious player among Western powers. An October 1905 mission-study lesson plan in the *Woman's Missionary Friend* acknowledged this new reality, indicating that when discussing Japan, it would be important to avoid "confusion in use of terms 'Western' and 'Christian' in alluding to modern civilization" (WFMS, *WMF,* 1905, 37, no. 10:358); Japan's victory over the Russians revealed that the triumphal power of modern civilizations was not confined to the "Christian West." American reactions to Japanese victories ranged from admiration of Japanese "advances" (an admiration that was often combined with an ideological tendency to downplay differences between Japan and the West) to outright fear and hostility toward the "yellow peril" of Japan.

Numerous scholarly texts were published during this era that sought to inform the Western world about the new reality of Japan's power. In *The Mastery of the Pacific* (1902), Archibald R. Colquhoun stated, "The Pacific Ocean is the arena for many young Powers—the young Australasia, the young America, the new Russia in the Far East, and not least the new Japan. . . . Of all the changes and developments, however, nothing is more sensational than that of Japan, and in the story of the Pacific the new Japan will certainly play a prominent part . . . . she shows . . . a determination to meet the West on its own ground, to enter the fields of rivalry, military and commercial, manufacturing and scientific" (367, 368). In light of the Japanese victory in their war against Russia, Henry Dyer, author of *Dai Nippon: The Britain of the East* (1904), stated that the lesson the West needed to "take to heart" was that

> in so far at least as Japan, China, and Korea are concerned, there must be a profound change in the methods of dealing with these nations. The

> days of crooked diplomacy, gunboat policy, veiled threats and monstrous indemnities must be looked upon as past, and all questions must be discussed and settled on a basis of international equality. . . . if the bogey of the "Yellow Peril" ever becomes a reality, it will be on account of the conduct of some of the Western Powers, whose aggressions will drive the peoples of the Far East into militarism. (429–30)

While thick, scholarly tomes like these were available to a serious reading public, missionary literature put this information in a format more easily accessible to a general audience. While anti-Japanese sentiments were growing in the early-twentieth-century United States, the *Woman's Missionary Friend* was an important disseminator of sympathetic images of Japan. During the Russo-Japanese War, one of its articles stated: "While every magazine, secular and church paper is supplying you with interesting material on Japan, there is no paper which takes the place of our *Woman's Missionary Friend.* This paper gives you the latest news from our work in Japan and every other field. Every woman in our society needs this magazine" (WFMS, *WMF,* 1905, 37, no. 2:57). The *Woman's Missionary Friend* made world events personal, as women who supported missions read about their missionaries' experiences with international developments. Most issues during the Russo-Japanese War were filled with personal stories of missionary women in Japan who witnessed the war efforts firsthand.

While the WFMS as an organization generally sought to promote the idea of "universal brotherhood" among all the world's people, during the Russo-Japanese War, missionary rhetoric in support of Japan was often framed in such a way that it did not fully challenge the notion of racial hierarchy but merely placed Japanese at the top of the hierarchy along with Caucasians. While WFMS coverage of the Sino-Japanese war ten years earlier had supported the Japanese, the complete loyalty to Japan that filled the pages of the *Woman's Missionary Friend* during the Russo-Japanese War was at an unprecedented intensity—and was even more striking in that missionaries repeatedly emphasized the superiority of the Japanese race over the Russians. WFMS literature on the war resonated with the rhetoric of Japanese leaders who sought to convince Americans that it was the Japanese who reflected the highest values and characteristics of the

West, not the Russians. The *Woman's Missionary Friend* even highlighted a statement from Japan's prime minister that the war was "analogous to that of ancient Greece in her contest with Persia. . . . Japan is Greece, and Russia is Persia"; the *WMF* added its own editorial comment that "Japan has certainly manifested some of the noblest characteristics of that early Republic" (WFMS, *WMF,* 1905, 37, no. 10:348).

Thus the WFMS followed the lead of Japanese politicians and their sympathizers who sought to convince the American public that it was Japan that was essentially "white" and "Christian," and it was Russia that represented heathendom. For example, as Joseph M. Henning discusses in *Outposts of Civilization,* a Japanese diplomat, Kaneko Kentarō, stated that Japan, "though Oriental, stands for modern western civilization, and its success will mean . . . the occidentalizing of the East. The other, though European, stands for an absolutism that is Oriental, and its success will mean the perpetuation of ignorance and the reign of force" (2000, 144). The president of the United States, Theodore Roosevelt, desiring a victory for Japan because he believed the Japanese government was more likely than Russia to maintain an open-door policy in Asia, advocated Kaneko's view (and even had Kaneko take a bearskin from one of his hunting expeditions to the Japanese emperor, symbolizing Russia's defeat) (Henning 2000, 144). Thus, from the highest echelons of American government to the most widely dispersed mission literature of the day, the Japanese had powerful allies in disseminating positive images of their country to the American public. The *Woman's Missionary Friend* gave American Protestant women a monthly dose of pro-Japan rhetoric; as one self-promotional piece in the magazine stated: "'I have a Friend, oh such a Friend'. . . . when she visited me in July she informed me that 'among the greatest naval battles ever fought was that of the Korean Straits, between Russia and Japan, the victory being overwhelmingly for Japan.' Also, 'Russia spends eight cents per capita on the education of her people; Japan with only one-eighth of Russia's revenue, spends thirty-four'" (WFMS, *WMF,* 1905, 37, no. 10:371).

The missionaries who wrote articles on their experiences in wartime Japan used a highly sentimental language, revealing a feeling near patriotism for their foreign home. "The war is a benefit," wrote missionary Georgiana Baucus, "in that it is disciplining and chastening this proud, high-spirited nation, as it has never been disciplined and chastened before. They have bowed their necks to the yoke of a long, arduous, exhausting struggle. What fortitude, what endurance, what powers of perseverance must result!" (WFMS, *WMF,* 1905, 37, no. 1: 5–6). The *Woman's Missionary Friend* thus portrayed Japan's war efforts in the way its American audience liked to think about their own country's militarism—as a reflection of a brave, noble, and even kind national character, sacrificing for the greater good of humanity. As an article by a Japanese woman stated, "Japan is fighting for the sake of peace, for liberty, civilization and the 'open door'" (17).

Missionaries reported that the Japanese treatment of Russian prisoners of war was "humane and generous"; one missionary stated that the "Japanese use rice as their staple food, but for the prisoners, who seem more like guests, they try to provide wheat bread and to furnish them the kind of food they would have at home." Many articles lauded the selfless sacrifices of Japanese for the war effort. For example, one of Elizabeth Russell's colleagues wrote, "In our Kwassui school, in Nagasaki, a patriotic society was formed which did noble work. . . . our girls made over one hundred comfort bags. . . . What noble patriotic girls they are!" (WFMS, *WMF,* 1905, 37, no. 10:373). One missionary even suggested that Japanese soldiers were better behaved than American soldiers, writing, "There were 30,000 soldiers in Nagasaki at one time, but I never saw but a single drunken one, but on a steamer passing through from the Philippines to the United States, one may count a dozen" (372). Another missionary highlighted the efficiency of the Japanese medical system that cared for the war wounded, proclaiming that "The simplicity and perfection of Japanese organization bode well for the future of the Christian church in this land" (WFMS, *WMF,* 1906, 38, no. 1:2).

In general, missionaries in Japan seem to have been completely in awe of the Japanese during this war, and they were not shy about showing this in their writings published in the *Woman's Missionary Friend.* One group of WFMS missionaries reported working with Japanese women to distribute rice cakes to soldiers as they were about to depart for war, and then raising their arms in the air and shouting "banzai!" along with the Japanese women as the soldiers' trains pulled out of the station (WFMS, *WMF,* 1905, 37, no. 4:116). At times this war excitement seems to have triggered in some of the missionaries a romantic longing for the soldiers. Georgiana Baucus and fellow WFMS missionary Emma Dickinson took on the ministry of visiting wounded soldiers in a military hospital, and both reported their immense delight in engaging with the young, receptive men. "Miss Dickinson remarked one day upon how white and refined the men's faces had grown through sickness," Baucus wrote, "so different from the ruddy, brawny sons of war we had seen depart a year ago." Having felt warmly welcomed by the men at the hospital, Baucus continued, "It is little wonder . . . that no missionary can be satisfied with only one visit. If she goes once, she must go again and again and again. . . . She is intoxicated as if she had been taking new wine" (WFMS, *WMF,* 1906, 38, no. 1:2, 3).

Dickinson was even more ecstatic than Baucus about visiting the wounded soldiers. With language that verged on the erotic, she wrote in an almost giddy article for the *Woman's Missionary Friend* that "[t]he days I cannot go [to the hospital], I feel every fibre of my being reaching out like the fibres of a running plant for *my* soldiers." One soldier, in particular, engaged in an intimate correspondence about spiritual matters with Miss Dickinson, and she treasured his notes like love letters; she wrote, "My desk now holds quite a pile of cards written in the same hand, and all holding some special word." She described his face as "full of natural refinement, which, added to the pitiful refinement of suffering, which is to be seen on all the faces in the pitiful place, made it almost angelic." When she went to visit "her soldier," she thrilled upon seeing "his big Testament . . . at the head of his bed." The Testament itself became a sensual object of their correspondence, according to Dickinson's description: "'It is so deep, and full,' he wrote me the other day, 'this Gospel, that I cannot take it in.'" Always after making rounds at the hospital, Dickinson wrote, "I take my way back to *my* soldier. Ah, *he* never disappoints me!" (WFMS, *WMF,* 1906, 38, no. 1:4, 5).

Amid this excitement during the Russo-Japanese War, a prominent strain in missionary literature, and in general American discourse, was that the Japanese, being so similar to Westerners that they were virtually white, were the key for bringing Western-style civilization to all of Asia.[3]

3. For a more in-depth analysis of this issue, see Henning's *Outposts of Civilization* (2000), ch. 6.

Numerous Americans shared Baucus's view that "[w]e certainly cannot do better than be vigilant in our efforts in Japan; for the more light there, the less darkness throughout the East!" (WFMS, *WMF,* 1906, 38, no. 8:276). Such discourses not only legitimated Western imperialism but Japanese imperialism in Asia as well.

Yet this rhetoric was tempered by competing discourses in mission literature that challenged notions of racial and cultural hierarchy. While missionaries in Japan were particularly attached to the Japanese, missionaries in India, China, the Philippines, various locales in Africa, and other countries also sought to represent their host cultures in ways that would diminish prejudices among their denominational supporters. A racist critic, unhappy about such influence in the United States, stated, "the missionaries in the different countries. . . . simply have a sympathetic identification with the country and the people they work with and that identification may become so perfect that they may oppose the interests and upturn the destiny of their homelands." Opposing the "interests of their homelands," in this critic's mind, included missionaries' support for "equal opportunity in white lands for all the races of the earth" (Flowers 1917, 167, 159).

Moreover, although numerous missionaries tended to support imperialism if they believed it would aid in the Christianization and social uplift of conquered lands, a growing strain of missionary discourse was becoming more critical of imperialism, even questioning whether Christianity and the militarism of powerful nation-states were compatible at all. Elizabeth C. Northup, who became editor of the *Woman's Missionary Friend* in 1905, indicated to her readers, for example, that "Christianity should not be identified with 'triumphant military force and successful commercial greed'" (WFMS, *WMF,* 1905, 37, no. 10:358). That same year, a Japanese student at a mission school in Hiroshima read an article from a Japanese newspaper to a group of missionaries, which stated, "Only when our fleet crushed the Russian fleet, and our army defeated the Russian army, did [Western powers] commence to take us seriously. . . . In other words, it is by virtue of our achievement in destruction, and not by that in construction, that we have been recognized as an equal among Occidental nations. We do not know whether or not this is a matter upon which we should congratulate ourselves." One of the Americans present at this recitation, William Elliott, published these words in *The Japan Evangelist,* in an article titled "Is Japan Civilized? Are We?" Commenting upon the Japanese article, Elliott stated that "the question here, that ought to force itself to the front in the heart of every American and European is, Have we been as careful as possible to eliminate from our civilization ideal the old 'savage,' Might-is-right spirit? Is the Western policy itself . . . at bottom really 'constructive' and not 'destructive'—firmly foundationed . . . on intelligent individual and universal justice and love . . . ?" (WFMS, *WMF,* 7, no. 2:64). Less than a decade later, an increasing number of Westerners, including American women involved in missions, began to ask such questions, as World War I shook modernized nation-states to their core.

Expanding Roles for Women

In the February 1907 issue of the *Woman's Missionary Friend,* an article titled "A Progressive School" highlighted Kwassui Jo Gakkō, stating, "Our Woman's Foreign Missionary Society school in Nagasaki has kept ahead of the old beliefs of Japan through the bold, statesman-like methods of Miss Elizabeth Russell. It was the pioneer school and has made a revolution in girls' schools. . . . [It] maintains a higher standard than the Woman's Japanese College." The article went on to point out that the Russo-Japanese War had brought "women into many official positions," and that schools like Kwassui could help to ensure that these positions were filled by "Christian graduates" (WFMS, *WMF,* 1907, 39, no. 2:55).

The evolving gender ideologies of the WFMS were implicitly revealed in this article. Carefully following the successes of missionaries such as Russell, women's missionary literature portrayed women's influence in the public sphere in a positive light, which stood in tension with the Victorian domestic ideal advocated in the early days of the women's mission movement. These competing visions stood side by side in the literature of the movement over the years, appealing to a spectrum of gender ideologies. Over time, the rhetoric of the movement began to resonate more and more with liberal American feminism. Ironically, in the early twentieth century, women's missionary literature often indicated that women's emancipation in the public sphere was a natural outcome of Western,

Christian influence, and that the social, economic, and political oppression of women was caused by "Oriental," heathen religion; the article on Kwassui highlighted the school's triumph over "the old beliefs of Japan," with no mention of the school's challenge to traditional American Protestant ideologies. Although numerous women involved in missions grew more sensitive about cultural difference over time, even to the extent that they opposed the use of the words "heathen" or "pagan" to describe non-Christian religions, they were in no hurry to stop calling the perceived degradation of women "heathenish." As Jean Miller Schmidt states, WFMS women were largely blind to "sources of women's power in other cultures and religious traditions" and often slighted "indigenous reform efforts" (1999, 177). By associating the subordination of women with heathendom and women's social liberation with true Christianity, white American women lifted up themselves through their movement to uplift the "other."

While the early women of the WFMS were careful not to challenge overtly the ideology of separate spheres for men and women, over time those involved in women's missions more openly defied the limitations placed upon their gender. As Patricia R. Hill discusses in *The World Their Household,* the growth of the women's mission movement "served as a bridge between the domestic sphere and the male-dominated arena of public life" as it boosted "women's estimation of themselves and their capabilities" (1985, 119). While there had been much trepidation about women's ability to carry out the administrative responsibilities for supporting missionaries and their work overseas, American Protestant women proved themselves to be more than capable. In 1874, an article in *The Heathen Woman's Friend* proudly reported: "Already several bodies of women support one hundred and ninety missionary ladies, with three hundred native helpers. . . . Of these, sixty missionaries are in India, thirty in Turkey, the others in China, Japan, Africa, Greece, Spain, Mexico, South America, Siam, Burmah, Persia, and with the North American Indians" (WFMS, *HWF,* 1873, 5, no. 6:575).

WFMS work in Japan, in particular, struck pride in Methodist women because, unlike other mission fields, they were involved in the original establishment of missions in that country along with the General Missionary

Society. Since the WFMS had been created several decades after the Methodist Church had begun work in foreign missions, when General Board missionaries were sent to places like China or India, WFMS missionaries usually arrived in a situation where missionary work had been more or less established and defined by the General Board. In Japan, however, the first missionaries from the General Board arrived only in 1873 and were followed the next year by WFMS missionary women. A decade later, a contributor to *The Heathen Woman's Friend* proudly highlighted the capabilities WFMS missionaries had shown in developing this new mission field, stating, "*When the Woman's Foreign Missionary Society entered the Island Empire, she had no Methodist constituency from which to draw workers.* Our Parent Board had occupied stations for but little more than a year, and the Methodist Episcopal Church had, perhaps, all told, about half a dozen members in a country where she now has a membership of nine hundred. The Woman's Society had *to help form a Christian Constituency.* She was a pioneer as well as the General Society" (WFMS, *HWF,* 1885, 16, no. 9:207; emphasis in original). Nothing could reveal more clearly to Methodists the ability of women to successfully engage in unchartered enterprises, independent of male guidance.

The very act of publishing and circulating their mission magazine foreshadowed how the movement would come to support American women's professionalization; as one leader of the women's mission movement remembered, when women's mission periodicals were first published in 1869, "papers and magazines conducted by women were something of a novelty, the field new and untried" (Baker [1896] 1987, 73–74). The women successfully produced and marketed their magazines, eventually circulating them to tens of thousands of subscribers. The women who were first involved in the movement even surprised themselves with their newly discovered abilities; as one woman exclaimed four years after the WFMS was founded, "How much talent has this infant society already called out! What able essays have been written and eloquent speeches made by women unused to this exercise of pen or tongue!" (WFMS, *HWF,* 1873, 5, no. 6:589).

Women involved in missions thus helped to advance women's careers in previously male-dominated arenas. Like other women's missionary organizations, the WFMS focus on female mission schools appealed to

Victorian understandings of proper women's work; yet from the very beginning the WFMS was also drawn into supporting mission work that would take women well beyond clearly established gender roles. Women in the medical profession grew in respectability, for example, as the WFMS responded to the call of missionaries in the field, who as early as 1869 indicated their "growing conviction, that a most urgent want . . . is found in a demand for female doctors" (WFMS, *HWF,* 1869, 1, no. 2:11). The WFMS benefitted from Sarah Josepha Hale's patronage of women's medical missions. Hale, the editor of *Godey's Lady's Book,* sought to make women's mission work and medical education as stylish as the latest fashions featured in her magazine. She founded the Ladies' Medical Society of Philadelphia in 1851, which offered to fund the medical education of women who would pledge themselves to the mission field. Hale's vision of women's medical missions was not fulfilled until the formation of the WFMS in 1869, when one of the women she had funded finally became a missionary (Hill 1985, 43–44). The WFMS appointed Dr. Clara Swain, a graduate of the Woman's Medical College of Pennsylvania, as its second foreign missionary (Hoskins 1912). Dr. Swain accompanied the WFMS's first appointed missionary, Isabella Thoburn, to India. Other female medical missionaries were soon appointed by the WFMS, and during the next fifty years the society sent out 147 women physicians (Robert 1996, 162).

While the WFMS continued its strong emphasis on the importance of women in the domestic sphere, a growing number of women in the movement were proud of their organization's role in lending a respectable status to women embarking on new paths for their gender. In discussing the controversy over women's medical education, one contributor to *The Heathen Woman's Friend* indicated that women's expanded sphere was "the finger of providence," stating that

> we have seen women seeking a higher culture, a fuller development, than had hitherto been afforded them. Some knocked at the door of medical colleges and asked admission, and great was the consternation and cry concerning it; and some of us did not know what all this meant, and why all this was. But soon the cry came from India,—send us women who can heal the sick as well as teach the ignorant and save the sinning. . . .

> Thus we read the "signs of the times" to be: this is woman's era, not for unwomanly claims and clamor, but for deeper devotion, fuller consecration, and growing out of these, more earnest and far-reaching activities. (WFMS, *HWF,* 1873, 4, no. 9:429)

Careful to distinguish women's missions from the negative stereotypes of the women's rights movement (by insisting that this was not about "unwomanly claims and clamor"), the article indicated that medical work would make a woman "more womanly, in being more like her Lord and Master, who went about doing good" (429). According to this logic, imitating Christ made one more womanly than more manly; indeed, women in the mission movement frequently co-opted elements of the masculine sphere (a male God; a male medical profession), claiming them for womanhood by feminizing them.

The women of the WFMS were also interested in working directly to "save souls" along with male missionaries. However, it was at this point that the WFMS was most adamantly opposed by men in their churches, for approval of women evangelists abroad would be tantamount to approving women preachers at home. Interestingly, the WFMS found that training native Bible women to become evangelists in their own countries met with less resistance from the General Board than appointing American women to be evangelists. As Dana L. Robert states, "public support for women evangelists lagged behind that for women teachers and doctors. . . . The first money raised by the Woman's Foreign Missionary Society for direct evangelistic work in 1869 was given to a native Bible woman, not to a western missionary with the title of 'evangelist'" (1996, 167).

Whether native women or American missionary women were doing evangelistic work, WFMS reports sometimes euphemistically labeled their activity in preaching the gospel as woman's work, detracting attention from the fact that they were actually doing something considered to be the direct opposite of women's work as they preached in the mission field. Nevertheless, the notion of women preaching was introduced to a broad American audience through the missionary movement. While the men of the General Board had insisted that women involved in missions should not engage in public speaking—much less public preaching—before mixed male and female audiences, WFMS literature continually chipped away at this ideological barrier over the years, with prominent male support. Early on, for example, Rev. James Thoburn, who was a great advocate not only of women's missions but also of women's public preaching, defied the men in his denomination who sought to silence the women, printing an article in *The Heathen Woman's Friend* in which he stated that the evangelical fervor of the women of the church was "the most wonderful religious phenomenon I have ever seen." Declaring that women involved in missions were "anointed with peculiar spiritual power," Thoburn stated, "One woman, who formerly shrank from the thought of speaking in a little class-meeting, now rises calmly to address a thousand hostile sinners. Another, who felt unable to teach in Sunday School, now travels a hundred miles to speak at a missionary meeting. . . . the old controversy concerning woman's right 'to speak in meeting' is smothered in an avalanche of convincing facts" (WFMS, *HWF*, 1876, 8, no. 5:103). Another piece announced:

> The brethren seem to think that "woman's work for woman" is likely to develop into woman's work for men and women. Thus Rev. Mr. Atkinson writes to the "Missionary Herald":
>
> "I am constrained to put in a cry for more women. Women as missionaries can do a work in Japan that women cannot do in other lands. . . . *Men* will listen to the women's words to women. They may not always be visible, though they often are; but Miss Talcott and Miss Dudley can tell of many male listeners just at the other side of only paper screens. Women can do large and good pastoral work. . . . Hence, dear brother, in your sendings out, send more women." (WFMS, *HWF*, 1875, 7, no. 2:25)

The experiences of missionary women in their "new sphere of usefulness" fueled the imagination of American Protestant women, as they lived vicariously through the stories and letters of missionary women printed in WFMS publications. Women's missionary literature was filled with stories of women's exciting travels in lands afar, carrying articles with titles like "From the Mediterranean to the Ganges" and "Scraps from a 20,000 miles Journey." Unmarried women in the mission field often expressed much satisfaction over their choice of career and communicated to women back in the United States their exceeding pleasure at their accomplishments and adventures. As one missionary woman stated, "The Lord has given me so much to be thankful for lately, that I would like to transfer a little of it to America, and let you share it with me." Suggesting that her call to a public life of missionary work was even more worthy than a life of motherhood and domesticity, another missionary woman wrote, "I feel quite sure there can be no happier person, nor any more blessed work than mine" (WBM, Fourth Annual Report, 1872, 8). Far from the martyred and pathetically unwed and childless women imagined by the early critics of the women's mission movement, missionary women communicated to women back in the United States that life in the public sphere as educated, skilled professionals could be successfully and rewardingly accomplished by women.

While there continued to be negative stereotypes of women involved in missions (as late as 1908, for example, one young woman stated that "her idea of a missionary meeting was a few lorn females, clad in black, sitting in a chill corner of a desolate church, singing 'Come, ye disconsolate'" [WFMS, *WMF,* 1908, 40, no. 11:384]), hundreds of thousands of American women found the mission movement to be enthralling, with "its fascinating possibilities, its splendid appeal to the heroic, its demands upon the highest capacity for steady, concentrated work, its rewards to mind and spirit" (WFMS, *WMF* 1907, 39, no. 6:203). According to the *Woman's Missionary Friend,* one could identify a woman involved in the mission movement, either as a missionary or as a supporter, by her broad, cosmopolitan world view—"her quick wit, her wide knowledge of current events, [and] her sympathetic insight into modern conditions" (203).

Women's Emancipation from Heathenish Patriarchy

In 1873, during the early years of the women's mission movement, an article in *The Heathen Woman's Friend* sarcastically stated, "The grand duty of a wife in this world, by which she alone can obtain happiness in a future state, is, *service* to her husband. This service consists in her entire obedience to his will, and in her solicitude and efforts at home to make him comfortable. . . . A woman is believed to be an inferior being, and has numerous disadvantages, social, mental, and religious" (WFMS, *HWF,* 1873,

4, no. 11:cover page). This was not a critique of women's limited place in American society, although it certainly could have been a description of prescribed social roles placed on American women of the day; instead, it was a condemnation of Hindu gender ideologies, serving as an example of the backward nature of non-Christian civilizations—it was in *heathendom* where the "family is patriarchal [and] [t]he father is the head" (WFMS, *HWF*, 1869, 1, no. 6:44), and where there was "social oppression and injustice exercised towards woman" (WFMS, *HWF*, 1869, 1, no. 2:9).

In the first decades of the women's mission movement, their literature was very careful to avoid criticisms of gender divisions within Western, "Christian" nations. Instead, the literature incessantly criticized the lack of rights of women in other cultures. This likely served as an indirect outlet for the frustration American women felt at their own powerlessness. It also served as a rhetorical strategy of suggesting that any subordination of women was heathenish and not to be sanctioned by true Christians. Thus, missionary rhetoric about other cultures indirectly challenged women's subordination in the West, at the expense of denigrating non-Western cultures. As the success of women in building an international missionary movement became an undeniable reality, however, women in charge of the enterprise became bolder in more directly supporting women's rights in the United States, rather than just by cataloguing the horrors of women's lives in "heathen" cultures.

In the first year *The Heathen Woman's Friend* was distributed, Methodist minister Rev. T. J. Scott contributed an article in which he proclaimed that "Christianity is eminently the friend of woman. . . . Save where Christianity has recognized her true character and relation, and has exalted and blessed her, she is ignorant, degraded, enslaved, and debarred from many of the privileges and enjoyments of life, accessible to the other sex" (WFMS, *HWF*, 1869, 1, no. 2:9). This was a central theme in women's missionary literature for years to come. At first, the elevation of American womanhood was linked to the Victorian ideology of domesticity; according to the rhetoric, Protestant women were blessed in that they had freedom in the home, were treated with respect by Protestant men, and had access to education, unlike women in heathen lands. "The Hindoo Shasters say: 'The supreme duty of a wife is to obey the mandate of her husband. . . .

A woman has no other god than her husband," an article in *The Heathen Woman's Friend* proclaimed. "Our Bible gives us the home,—that one sweet bit of paradise that has survived the fall. Dare we, Christian women, withhold the cup of cold water from those who perish with thirst?" (WFMS, *HWF,* 1874, 6, no. 5:749).

However, in this rhetoric about the uplift of women through Christianity, there was significant slippage between linking women's religious emancipation with domestic bliss and linking it with the full equality of the sexes. Another article contrasting Hinduism and Christianity indicated that there was a biblical mandate for transcending gender hierarchy: "A missionary asked an intelligent Brahmin why his people treat their wives with such marked indifference and neglect. 'Because,' was the reply, 'our sacred books teach us that the woman is an impure being.' Now listen to one of the basal truths of Christianity! 'There is neither male nor female, but ye are all one in Christ Jesus'. . . . Christianity is the woman's Magna Charta" (WFMS, *HWF,* 1870, 1, no. 8:69). Over the years, American women in mission took the credit for women's entry into public arenas around the world, as mission literature highlighted this as a sign that Christianity was in fact influencing non-Christian cultures. A 1907 issue of the *Woman's Missionary Friend* featured an article on progress in China, which began with the quip: "'A girl is no good—only to get married.' Familiar? Oh, no, that's 'heathen Chinese,' not even modern China." While the heathen China of the past had no roles for women to play other than wife and mother, the article proclaimed, as a result of mission schools—"each burning a hole in the dark that is causing the whole system of heathenism to break into pieces"—the women of modern China now had a number of new paths open to them. In particular, the article highlighted Chinese graduates of female mission schools who went on to study medicine in the United States, returning to work in China as doctors (WFMS, *WMF,* 1907, 39, no. 4:115, 117). In another article that year, titled "The New Woman in China," Rev. John Parker wrote about how some Chinese young women "now dress in almost the same cut of clothes as men" in order to be able to freely walk the streets and take "the same studies as their brothers," noting that the "fashionable small feet . . . had disappeared, and the fair student[s] wore top boots." Preferring this "gender bending" over the tradition of binding feet,

Reverend Parker recounted how the missionaries were "rather amused" that they could not tell the difference between their male students and "these Amazons" and ended his story by exclaiming, "What a wonderful change for China!" (WFMS, *WMF*, 1907, 39, no. 10:364).

By the end of World War I, Christian converts who were career women were unabashedly displayed in the pages of the *Woman's Missionary Friend*. An 1918 article titled "The Emancipation of the Women of the East" included two photographs of attractive young women with the captions "A Progressive Woman of the Philippines—The Only Woman in the Orient Who Earns Her Living by Practicing Law at the Bar" and "A Business-Trained Korean College Graduate." The article quoted historian Tyler Dennett's book *The Democratic Movement in Asia*, highlighting Dennett's firm conviction that "'the Filipina woman is one of the greatest apologetics for Christianity in the Orient. She is today so far in advance of her other Oriental sisters in freedom, social position and independence that she is in a class by herself,' because Christianity has for years been rooted in the Philippines." While admitting that Spanish colonialism in the Philippines (though not the succeeding colonial rule of the United States) had been "unprogressive," the article claimed that the "Christian valuation of womanhood" had somehow filtered through the brutality of colonial rule. The article also stated that because of Christianity, a "spirit of rebellion is working among the Japanese, who are refusing to be kept at home practicing obedience to their husbands and fathers," and that in China "one will find plenty of high spirited feminists in the mission schools" (WFMS, *WMF*, 1918, 50, no. 11:380–81).

Suffrage

The feminist movement in the United States had long faced powerful opposition from Christian leaders, but, as architects of women's rights campaigns were well aware, they needed the support of Christians if they were going to be successful in altering American laws and culture. Although the early women's mission movement appropriated prevailing gender ideologies and was often outwardly unsympathetic to the women's rights movement—portraying those who sought political rights as selfish and unwomanly—women's experiences in the missionary movement ultimately strengthened the women's rights movement in the United States. As the image of the missionary woman working to uplift the status of women around the world became an acceptable trope in the minds of middle-class Protestant Americans, the suffrage movement began to find more widespread acceptance as well.

WFMS support for women's rights was often indirect and restrained, yet this approach was effective in eventually eroding American Protestants' distaste for feminism. Just as Methodist women had found it necessary to be diplomatic in their interactions with the men of the General Mission Board who sought to limit their scope of activity in order to organize their independent women's missionary society, for years the WFMS found it politic not to ruffle feathers in their denomination by focusing too boldly on the explosive issue of women's rights. The cause of women's rights had prominent opponents in the Methodist world; James Monroe Buckley, for example, the influential editor of the Methodist Episcopal periodical *The Christian Advocate* from 1880 to 1912, cautioned in one of his 1891 editorials that women who campaigned for expanded rights in religious and civic arenas would bring down the wrath of God. He stated that "[i]mperious women, cursing the day they were born because they were not made men, have rebelled against their own nature, and therefore against God's law. Ambitious women, seeking to rival men, because they cannot bear to see them possess a kind of power denied to them, have sought to wrest dominion. . . . [they] have sought pre-eminence through means condemned by the law of God" ([1891] 1987, 11).

Criticizing Frances Willard and the Women's Christian Temperance Union (WCTU) for championing, like "infidels," the women's suffrage cause among the church people, Buckley derided the WCTU for trying to draw the WFMS into its suffrage campaign ([1891] 1987, 25). Declaring that "every man who understands the Gospel finds no difficulty in wishing his wife, mother, sister, and daughter to be subject to himself and other men in the sense in which the Gospel requires it," Buckley warned his Methodist audience that the moment women gained equal rights in Church and society, "the *Christian family* is gone" (11, 17). According to Buckley, women who truly sought to promote Christianity and the family would accept biblical mandates regarding women's silence and obedience, and acknowledge that theirs was "a noble sort of disenfranchisement," which included the "right" to "live under the protection of a stronger arm than her own. . . . and to look to that head to plan for her well-being" (26, 14).

The leaders of the WFMS decided that their official position would be to claim "no partisanship in politics," declaring that "its workers on the field are too far away to feel any of the heart-burnings of the political fray!" (WFMS, *WMF*, 1907, 39, no. 1:13). Yet it is clear that from the beginning some individuals involved in the WFMS did not agree with Buckley's position, and WFMS support for women's emancipation became increasingly evident over time, as their passionate denouncements of women's lack of rights in other countries indicated. Moreover, the literature of the WFMS frequently highlighted the activities and words of Methodists and other prominent Protestants who did in fact support women's suffrage. Not all leading men of the Methodist Episcopal Church opposed the women's rights movement; this was, in part, why the issue was so contentious in the denomination, and why individuals like Buckley were driven to write such defensive editorials in support of patriarchy.

The Heathen Woman's Friend reprinted at length the words of one of the most prominent Methodists of the nineteenth century, MEC bishop Matthew Simpson, who was a strong supporter of both women's suffrage and women's missions. Bishop Simpson—who had been a friend of President Abraham Lincoln and had given the assassinated president's funeral address in 1865—regularly corresponded with the likes of Susan B. Anthony, Julia Ward Howe, and Lucy Stone, all leaders in the women's rights movement, as they solicited him to speak or send statements to be read at their suffrage conventions. He also worked with WCTU leader Frances Willard. As Lucy Stone wrote to him: "Your wide and weighty influence in & out of the powerful denomination which you so ably represent make your name one of the most efficient ones in the Country and we want it to stand . . . in connection with the great principle of Impartial & Universal suffrage. . . . This great cause *waits* for the religious influence to be thrown in its favor" (Stone 1869 and 1874).

Simpson supported women's suffrage for the same reason he supported women's missions; in a speech titled "Woman Suffrage," delivered on February 7, 1873, he asserted that women had a purifying and refining influence on social morality, both in the United States and abroad (Simpson 1873). When the WFMS was formed, Simpson's wife, Ellen Simpson, was one of the vice presidents of the organization, and Bishop and Mrs. Simpson had a prominent influence on the society in its early years. Bishop Simpson's support for suffrage was one of the only direct references to the controversial issue in the pages of *The Heathen Woman's Friend* during the early years of WFMS work; an 1871 issue of the WFMS magazine printed a speech Bishop Simpson delivered to the New York branch of the society, in which he stated that the work of the WFMS to build their organization, despite the controversy it sparked, was not so different from other efforts for women to find an elevated place in society. "Woman has been steadily winning her way," Simpson stated, "and in every instance she has been doing it in opposition to conservative views." Boldly, Simpson proclaimed to the women of the WFMS that "God is intending, evidently, that woman shall do something in this age more than in the past. . . . For more than a score of years I have believed that the full reformation of society would not come without the ballot for woman" (WFMS, *HWF*, 1871, 2, no. 7:78).

The WFMS magazine also highlighted other prominent prosuffragists. The magazine had frequent contributions from James W. Bashford—another Methodist Episcopal bishop and a missionary to China—who supported women's rights with the publication of pamphlets such as "The Bible for Woman Suffrage." The magazine closely followed the work of prosuffrage WCTU leader Frances Willard, who, as Jean Miller Schmidt has stated, "was a major influence in the redefinition of the image of True Christian Womanhood to include enfranchisement" (1999, 156). Perhaps most importantly, the WFMS heavily promoted the work of Helen Barrett Montgomery, the "principal spokeswoman for the [women's mission] movement in the twentieth century" (Hill 1985, 117).[4] In her extensive publications, Montgomery openly affirmed movements to bring about greater economic, political, and educational freedoms for women, including the prosuffragist women's rights movement, and connected these movements

4. For more on Helen Barrett Montgomery, see Abbott 1997; Cattan 1972; and Montgomery 1940.

to the work of the women's foreign mission movement to raise women's status around the world. While their literature did not overtly advocate women's rights, by encouraging Methodist women to read Montgomery's publications, as well as to attend the summer mission camps that she ran and to attend her lectures as she toured the country, the WFMS made sure that their constituency embraced a major spokesperson for women's political advancement.

Montgomery had had close ties with Susan B. Anthony for years, as both women lived and worked in Rochester, New York. Montgomery was a member of the Women's Political Equality Club of Rochester, and she had worked with Anthony to create the Woman's Educational and Industrial Union of Rochester in 1893, as well as to raise funds to open the University of Rochester to women students. In 1899, Montgomery was the first woman to be elected to public office in Rochester when voters put her on the town's school board. In her article titled "Equal Suffrage," which was published on the front page of *Harper's Bazar* in 1894, Montgomery argued for the ballot, using rhetoric similar to that used by Protestant women to garner support for their independent mission organizations: "The movement. . . . is not the attempt to storm the fortress of an enemy, but to re-enforce the ranks of friends. . . . The keynote of the agitation is not rights, but duties; not the exploiting of wrongs, but the acceptance of responsibilities. . . . [The movement] numbers . . . thousands of happy women, who have never felt in their own sheltered lives the slightest pressure of unjust discrimination; who desire the reform because they recognize the needs of less fortunate women" (Montgomery 1894, 354).

According to Montgomery, the suffrage movement—just like the women's mission movement—was not about white, middle-class women gaining rights for themselves, but a movement to help the less fortunate, as well as an attempt to "re-enforce the ranks" of the men of their class in constructing the ideal society. In Montgomery's mind, the campaign for women's rights was but an extension of women's missionary work because, for her, both were about reshaping the world according to middle-class Protestant values.

Montgomery, who served as the president of the Woman's American Baptist Foreign Mission Society from 1914 to 1924, was perhaps more passionate about the women's foreign mission movement than any other movement of her day. She heavily promoted the view that women's rights were a natural outgrowth of true Christianity. In *Western Women in Eastern Lands* (1910), her best-selling book celebrating the fiftieth-year jubilee of women's foreign mission work—and a book studied by women in all the major Protestant denominations—Montgomery stated that Christian progress throughout the nineteenth century was evident in that

> [a]ll the demands made by that ridiculed and persecuted little band of women [i.e., women's rights supporters], in their first convention at Seneca Falls, have since been adopted and embodied in law, save one only. They asked for woman the right to have personal freedom, to acquire an education, to earn a living, to claim her wages, to own property, to sue and be sued, to make contracts, to testify in court, to obtain a divorce for just cause, to possess her children, to claim a fair share of the accumulations during marriage, *to vote.* (9–10, emphasis in original)

Montgomery argued that the values and objectives of the women's rights movement were synonymous with those of the women's missionary movement—in short, the elevation of women. Implying a biblical basis for women's rights, she argued that if more missionary women explicitly took up the cause of women's rights, they would further their goals in mission work, for if "women fully recognized the emancipatory nature of the pure religion of Jesus, the force of the religious missionary arguments would be tremendously strengthened" (Montgomery 1910, 45).

While Montgomery admitted that "there are terrible wrongs against women in our own land," the difference between "Christian" America and non-Christian lands, she claimed, was that "the wrongs of Hindu, Chinese, and Moslem women are buttressed behind the sanctions of religion, and are endorsed by the founders of their faith; while in our own land these wrongs flaunt themselves against the spirit and the plain provisions of our religion" (Montgomery 1910, 45). Montgomery went on to say, "Strictly speaking, there is no Christian nation, but only nations in process of becoming Christian. But even so, the steady pressure of Bible ideals, exerted slowly and against tremendous difficulties, has already brought a revolution in the position of women" (69).

Dismissing the Pauline epistles' injunctions against women's leadership—so important to conservative Christians like James Monroe Buckley—as "not at all inspired" and merely "a stumbling block to so many," Montgomery instead emphasized, like many WFMS women, the apostle Paul's words in Galatians 3:28 as "the Magna Charta of womanhood in a Christianity in which there is neither male nor female" (Montgomery 1910, 72, 73). Linking women's evangelistic movements with women's rights campaigns, Montgomery had a grand vision—which ultimately became the vision of most women involved in the major Protestant denominations' missionary enterprises—to bring all people, regardless of national boundaries, into "Christ's great democracy" (73).

Disillusionment with the West

While mainstream American Protestant women made an ideological shift during the high decades of the mission movement, as their Victorian-era ideology of domesticity was eroded by a new focus on women's emancipation in the public sphere, their rhetoric, at least until World War I, continued to be optimistic about the ability of Westerners to "conquer the world for Christ." At the same time, a growing appreciation for non-Western cultures as a result of missions stood in tension with Protestants' enthusiasm for cultural imperialism, as it began to make thoughtful Americans involved in the movement more critical of their own ethnocentrism. The shock of World War I, followed by the United States' Immigration Act of 1924, would cause many mission-minded Americans to lose their certainty of the West's superiority. By the 1920s, many Methodist women had moved away from the ideological positions that had first fueled their mission movement, as the Victorian valorization of domesticity and Western imperialism (at least in its more overt forms) no longer resonated with their reshaped Christian vision.

Missions historian Andrew Walls has stated that in "the high days of the missionary movement Christianity was associated with a particular form of civilization and an advanced technology. . . . The association is now much less obvious. . . . [T]he confident assertions that Christians once made about the gospel-associated blessings of technology [and Western civilization] have given place to doubts of its efficiency, consciousness of its demonic power for destruction, and desire for its control" (1996, 237–38). World War I was certainly a major factor in changing missionary attitudes about Western civilization.

World War I horrified WFMS women and made them bolder in criticizing male-dominated Western power structures. Elizabeth Russell reflected the disgust WFMS women felt about this war when she wrote to Emma Tolbert, "How cheap men's lives are in the eyes of Emperors & Kings." An October 1914 editorial in the *Woman's Missionary Friend* aptly stated that the "outbreak of a stupendous world war has shocked men and women into sober-mindedness and re-adjustments of thought and feeling" (WFMS, *WMF,* 46, no. 10:354). The WFMS was alarmed that the war was fundamentally challenging their message to the world: that "Christianity exert[ed] a stronger moral imperative than Buddhism, or Mohammedanism." The editorial raised the question of the day: "Does [Christianity] keep Christian nations from flying at one another's throats and plunging millions of innocent men and women and little children into the horrors and agonies of war?" Never resolving this troubling problem, the author, not knowing the future, gave thanks to God that the United States had not entered the war, proclaiming that now "the obligation [was] laid upon citizens of the one great Christian nation that is not at war, to keep unsullied the cross of Christ before the eyes of the Orient" (354). In 1917, however, when the United States entered the war, all of the so-called Christian nations were, in the view of WFMS women, sullying the cross of Christ.

The war had the effect of driving women involved in the WFMS to embrace more political stances—not only stances that claimed political responsibilities for women, but also stances that called into question the powerbrokers of the Western world. One article decried men's misuse of their power, stating: "To-day, the world over, men still hold the ultimate decision of controversies between nations by hazard of war. . . . The underlying *credo* [of war] is a blasphemy against all our higher instincts, being simple, might makes right." The author sought to mobilize Methodist women politically so that they would challenge the misjudgments of the world's male leaders: "Let the Christian women of this and all lands unite in a fervent, persistent protest against war. . . . Have we the power? . . .

Let women's work in missions answer. Here has been shown the fidelity to Christ and his commands . . . which attest woman's capacity for high achievement, her earnestness of devotion to a selfless cause" (WFMS, *WMF,* 1915, 47, no. 5:164).

In another article titled "Two Holy Wars," China missionary Laura M. White—declaring herself a suffragist in the piece, revealing an erosion of WFMS restraint in overtly proclaiming political platforms—stated that the "female principle" in creation was "the nobler of the two, the prototype . . . of love itself." The male principle, in contrast—as exemplified by the war in Europe—was focused on "ambition, power and selfish interests, bringing death to millions." For White, the women's mission movement was a holy war on the side of life. Scoffing at those who would nationalistically pray for success at war, White asserted, "I cannot believe that the Prince of Peace smiles a blessing on any airship while it is raining hell out of his very heaven, or that the God of Love ever breathes his benediction on a battleship engaged in making thousands of 'children orphans, and widows desolate.' But I know that God blesses our women's forces by land and sea and air" (WFMS, *WMF,* 1915, 47, no. 5:9–10).

Once the United States was in the war, the women of the WFMS sought to show their sympathy for American soldiers and their families but continued to insist that true Christians should spurn the "selfish exclusivism that seeks only the advancement of one's own land." They also sought to convince Methodist women that "[w]e can best show love for our native land as we see it in its relation to all other lands and work for the common uplift of all" (WFMS, *WMF,* 1918, 50, no. 5:154). During the war, some WFMS women began to develop a more critical suspicion of the so-called benevolent intentions of imperialism. In one article about a province of China becoming a protectorate of Japan, earlier enthusiasm about Japan's growing power in the East was significantly tempered; the author stated, "Japan claims to be acting wholly in the interests of China. . . . The friends of Japan look to her to keep her promises, but they are also sadly aware that Christian nations, which are still far from being nations of Christians, have not invariably set her a good example" (WFMS, *WMF,* 1915, 47, no. 7:242). While other articles in the *Woman's Missionary Friend* continued to promote the imperialist notion of "the white man's [and woman's] burden" to save other cultures from themselves through Western control and influence, during World War I a growing strain of Protestant missionary literature revealed a distrust of the militaristic nation-states that had formerly been viewed as allies in fostering an age of universal brotherhood among the world's people.

After the war, the WFMS embraced the passage of the nineteenth amendment to the U.S. Constitution in 1920, which enfranchised American women. Fully politicized by this point, the *Woman's Missionary Friend* informed Methodist women that since they had "learned through bitter and bloody experience that women must do their part in making a warless world," there was no reason that "their votes and voices should not register their unequivocal opposition to the futility and the insanity of war." Calling on Methodist women to work for "the creation and enforcement of good laws" that would foster "world peace and world friendship," the magazine declared that "[e]very missionary and every supporter of missions is an internationalizing agency and an active factor in the creation of the will to peace" (WFMS, *WMF*, 1924, 56, no. 5:169–70).

After World War I, the Immigration Act of 1924 further horrified missionaries, as it was a major setback in their decades-long battle against white American ethnocentrism. For half a century, missionaries had been fighting anti-immigrant fervor in the United States. Since the nineteenth century, missionaries, especially those with connections to China, had been protesting anti-Chinese laws in the United States, and as the twentieth century began, missionaries had become alarmed as anti-Japanese sentiments now built toward additional restrictive legislation, as evidenced by the 1905 formation of the Asiatic Exclusion League in San Francisco. Part of the logic of missionary rhetoric during the Russo-Japanese War had been to convince Americans that the Japanese did not represent a yellow peril by insisting that Japanese were virtually white. While such rhetoric did little to tackle the larger problem of American racism, missionaries hoped to bolster the claims of Japanese immigrants in the United States that they were eligible for citizenship, which U.S. law at the time reserved only for whites and individuals of African descent (Henning 2000, 161). Just as China missionary Esther E. Baldwin had argued in 1881 that "the Chinese to-day are the most industrious, quiet, honest, sober, patient, and forbearing (oh, how forbearing!) immigrants in this land" ([1881, 1890] 1993, 149) and thus deserved treatment equal to white Americans, Japan missionaries portrayed Japanese as model citizens possessing a self-restraint that would put even Anglo-Saxons to shame.

Nevertheless, the anti-Japanese movement gained momentum in the next two decades, and Japanese were not deemed white by American courts of law. Even though President Theodore Roosevelt had supported Japan's victory in the Russo-Japanese War, as a result of the racial turmoil in California he negotiated a "Gentlemen's Agreement" with the Japanese government in 1907, in which Japanese laborers desiring to immigrate to the United States would no longer be issued passports. In 1913, California passed a law denying Japanese immigrants the right to land ownership.

By the 1910s, missionaries were becoming more organized in their efforts to change American prejudices against nonwhite immigrants to the United States. In fact, as Izumi Hirobe points out in *Japanese Pride, American Prejudice*, "the Protestant clergy, especially those who had formerly been missionaries in Japan" were the first to create "organizational movements directed against the anti-Japanese movement" in the States (2001, 5). Sidney Lewis Gulick, a former missionary to Japan who had taught at a Christian school in Kyoto, was a prominent leader of this cause, establishing the National Committee for Constructive Immigration Legislation and the Commission on Relations with Japan (5). As anti-Japanese fervor was reaching a fever pitch, Methodists distributed sympathetic literature about Japan to study groups in churches around the country, and the *Woman's Missionary Friend* urged its readers to "bring to the study minds unbiased by what we have read and heard of the 'Japanese peril,'" reminding them that their missionaries had made an "emphatic appeal for America to trust Japan. . . . Let us then approach the study . . . in a spirit of desire really to understand our neighbor across the Pacific and those of her sons and daughters who have come to our shores" (WFMS, *WMF*, 1923, 55, no. 6:208).

In 1917, prominent anti-Japanese propagandist Montaville Flowers published *The Japanese Conquest of American Opinion*, which heavily attacked the work of Gulick and like-minded Protestants, blaming "missionary enthusiasm" for giving white Americans the false impression that this "yellow race" could live harmoniously in what he saw as a white, Christian nation (165). He stated that revolutionary American notions of equality and human rights only made sense when they were applied to the men who founded the republic and their descendants, because these men "were the warp and woof of a new human fabric woven from the richest materials of the superior nations of the white race" (201). Moreover, Japanese religion, according to Flowers, made it impossible for them to conform to American values. "In Shintoism," Flowers proclaimed, "there is no concept to correspond to our idea of deity . . . [the] vast space which deity fills in our life is blank in theirs. . . . The Emperor . . . occupies the center of their devotion, for his ancestry is supreme. He is the direct descendant of Amaterasu the virgin *goddess* who married the Sun" (173–74, emphasis in the original). Highlighting these "pagan" features of Japanese religion, Flowers warned that the masses of Japanese were a threat to American Christianity, noting that the "sentimental admiration which some Americans have for Japan has already compromised their attitude toward pagan rites" (177). Arguing that missionaries to Japan were dangerously liberalizing American Protestants' views of the Japanese, he warned his readers to spurn the missionary claim that "the United States can adopt, rear and assimilate the Asiatic peoples." Mocking the claim of missionaries such as Sidney Gulick that the Japanese were no different than whites, Flowers warned that the commingling of Asian and white blood was a clear and present danger because "[n]o great human stock has come out of a radical race cross," and "[w]herever the white race has attempted to cross a pigmented race, it has lost its racial characteristics and lowered its civilization" (222). Such rhetoric won the day, and the Immigration Act of 1924, with its clause excluding any "alien ineligible to citizenship," became the law of the land. The exclusion clause of this act made it virtually impossible for anyone from Asia to emigrate to the United States and was clearly an attack on the Japanese people, as earlier laws had already restricted the immigration of people from other Asian nations.

Missionaries protested the act and strove to live according to their growing conviction that the Japanese and others were their equals. The 1924 annual report of the WFMS missionaries in Japan, distributed to their supporters in the United States, began with "A Plea for Understanding," which proclaimed: "Your missionaries in Japan, who for many years have been the recipients of countless kindnesses and courtesies from all classes of people, who have observed the high sense of honor—the trustworthiness and the devotion of their Japanese friends, cannot but be grieved to have this sensitive people wounded by what appears to them to be unnecessarily humiliating and unjust legislation. . . . One purpose of this report is to help the Methodist women of America to know and appreciate their Christian sisters in Japan" (MEC, Minutes of the Woman's Conference, 1924).

That same year, the General Conference of the Methodist Church, heavily influenced by its decades-long relationship with Japan through its missionaries, sent a letter of protest to President Calvin Coolidge, stating that "[a]s Christians, we cannot countenance racial prejudice and discrimination" (reprinted in Foner 1993, 159). The leaders of the WFMS announced in the *Woman's Missionary Friend* their "agreement with the pronouncement of the General Conference" and sent their own resolution to President Coolidge. Fully cognizant of the voting block their constituency now represented since American women had gained suffrage, the document stated that "the Executive Committee of the Woman's Foreign Missionary Society of the Methodist Episcopal Church, representing more than 600,000 American women, requests a reconsideration of this Exclusion Act with a view to eliminating race discrimination and to re-establishing the bonds of friendship that will make possible coöperation in works of peace throughout the world" (1924, 56, no. 12:436–37). As they had decried the ethical failings of Western nations during World War I, the women of the WFMS now voiced their disappointment with the United States in particular, as they asked themselves "What has become of . . . [the] spirit of Christian brotherhood?"

In 1924, American Protestant women, fully embracing their new political role in the world, organized an institute at Vassar College that brought together members of the League of Women Voters, the Federation of Women's Clubs, the Young Women's Christian Association, the Woman's Christian Temperance Union, the Council of Women for Home Missions, and the Federation of Women's Boards of Foreign Missions. The purpose of the gathering was "to discover the underlying causes that now prevent world relations on a Christian basis." Focusing on "the barriers—racial, economic, political," the goal of the meeting was to try "to find how to remove them" (WFMS, *WMF,* 1924, 56, no. 8:285). The mission-affiliated women comprised the largest group at the conference and they "registered many definite proposals for action," including listening to the recommendations of nonwhite women, as well as apologizing to them for Western, white arrogance. The author of the report from the institute was at pains to emphasize that "Mrs. Haynes and other prominent Negro women were members of the institute and valued participants in discussions" (287); and the women at the institute followed through with the missionaries' suggestions by sending "a cablegram through Madam Yajima to the women of Japan expressing deep regret over the present strained relations between the United States and Japan, and pledging united effort to promote . . . the principles of justice."

Missionary women led the way in complicating and deepening white Protestant Americans' thinking about race and gender. While they never shed the core of their faith—the belief in the superiority of Christianity—missionaries often modeled for their denominations how to shed elements of the ideologies and practices of white supremacy and patriarchy. In the first decades of the twentieth century, Methodist missionaries began to give the reins of control over the organizations they had created in countries around the world to converts who were citizens of those countries. As one editorial in the *Woman's Missionary Friend* stated, their objective had been to create "a church in India shaped for India's needs and type of mind; a church in Japan that is Japanese in its psychology and polity; a church in China suited to the Chinese; and each with self-government and self support." In this vein, as the report from the Vassar Institute noted, politicized Protestant women believed that their mission work could pave the way for new, improved "international relations" (WFMS, *WMF,* 1924, 56, no. 8:287).

As early as 1907, the Methodist Church of Japan was created through the merger of the Canadian Methodist Church, the Methodist Episcopal Church, and the Methodist Episcopal Church, South. The General Conference of the new organization elected a Japanese bishop, the Rev. Honda Yoitsu, who had been active in the Methodist Episcopal Church since the 1870s (Cary [1909] 1993, 122, 340). Elizabeth Russell, in a letter to the *Woman's Missionary Friend,* revealed how the event had symbolized the way Methodists had begun to transcend boundaries of national identity and gender. While only a few years earlier the MEC had been embroiled in controversy over whether women could be delegates to their General Conference in the United States, Russell "had the honor of election as delegate to the [first] General Conference" of the Methodist Church in Japan in 1907. She reported that there was "a fine feeling between Japanese and foreigners. . . . The election of the Bishop [Honda], his consecration, his introduction to the Conference as the new Bishop, were occasions that will linger long in the memories of all who were present" (WFMS, *WMF,* 1907, 39, no. 10:362).

While the percentage of Christians in Japan would continue to remain small, especially compared to the massive growth of Christianity in places like Korea or sub-Saharan Africa, in 1924 missionaries in Japan reported that the "day prayed for by missionaries the world over has now come in Japan, where . . . the burdens of administration can largely pass to the native people themselves, and the American worker . . . can now be free to stand shoulder to shoulder with the Japanese colleague" (WFMS, *WMF,* 1924, 56, no. 8:276). Another article that year featured the work of Methodist Japanese women at the mission schools Elizabeth Russell and Jennie Gheer had founded in Nagasaki and Fukuoka. The missionary author stated, "Throughout the year we work together, Japanese and foreigners alike. There is no East nor West to our thinking. We are all one . . . having an equal vote on all conference matters pertaining to the field. . . . The work of our conference is greatly strengthened by the presence of these Japanese women, who are missionaries together with us in bringing the life of God into the heart of the Empire of the Rising Sun" (WFMS, *WMF,* 1924, 56, no. 6:196–97). By the 1920s, many missionaries no longer saw Christianity as part and parcel of Western civilization. Their religion was taking on a new light, as it was becoming a part of the non-Western world. Their encounter with Japan influenced many American Protestant women to embrace a "Christian internationalism based on mutual respect, understanding and coöperation" (WFMS, *WMF,* 1924, 56, no. 11:391).

Epilogue

> O women of '22, we of '69 are here to welcome you. . . .
>
> [W]e set out on the long, long quest. Men laughed and sneered, they taunted and jeered. "What," said they, "you'll go on that wild search? You'll never reach the end. The way's too long, the road's too rough. You'll never have money enough. You can't; you can't!" said they. "We must and we will," said we. . . .
>
> We of '69 have blazed the trail, we have chosen the site, we have cleared the forest. It is yours, O women of '22, to build. You will build the world anew; you'll build it strong, you'll build it right.
>
> —"Greetings of Mrs. 1869," *Woman's Missionary Friend,* May 1922

American Protestant women's mission movements were full of contradictions and competing visions: they promoted both conservative gender ideologies and women's emancipation; both Western imperialism and ideals of racial equality. When Methodist women organized their independent missionary society in 1869, they set the women of America's largest Protestant denomination on a path that would ultimately challenge and complicate their cherished ideologies of civilization and gender. Protestant women who engaged in missions during the age of empire were part of a process by which the world was reshaped so that now, in the words of Edward Said, "all cultures are involved in one another; none is single and pure, all are hybrid, heterogenous, extraordinarily differentiated, and unmonolithic" (1993, xxv).

By the time the era of white women's missions was winding down in the 1920s, the movement had come to be comprised of individuals who were relatively progressive in their thinking, compared to many other Euro-Americans of their day. The succeeding generations of white women in mainline Protestant denominations would later engage with civil rights movements, the second wave feminist movement, and the revolutions of decolonization in the countries where Protestants had established missions. The more progressively minded among them would learn that white, Protestant Americans still had a long way to go in revising their ideologies of race, class, and gender, in order to be involved in the creation of a just world. The relationships between white women and women of color continue to be shaped by the troubled history of imperialism, which, as Nupur Chaudhuri and Margaret Strobel have stated, includes "any relationship of dominance and subordination between nations, including the modern form of economic control" (1992, 2), and by the related ideology of Orientalism, which Said has described as "a Western style for dominating, restructuring, and having authority over the Orient" (1979, 3). White, Western women have been intimately involved in the history and ideology of imperialism through their "complicity and resistance to dominant cultural values" (Chaudhuri and Strobel 1992, 6). Every generation has struggled with the flawed legacies of their foremothers, as they have sought to make the world "right."

As for Elizabeth Russell, her decision to go overseas as a missionary transformed her life. When interviewed at age ninety-one, shortly before her death, "she laughed when . . . she told of her narrow world horizon on that eventful day, October 25, 1879, which saw her sailing from her homeland to faraway enchanted Japan" (Johnson 1929, 112). After becoming a seasoned missionary in the field, one admirer stated that "[h]er interests were broad and she looked at all problems from a global point of view" (Couch n.d.).

By the time Russell retired in 1919, she was highly respected not only among Japanese but also by the foreign settlement in Nagasaki. Before her final departure she was decorated with the Japanese emperor's blue ribbon

May Russell with friends in the United States, ca. 1900. Courtesy of Kwassui Women's College.

medal in recognition of her educational and social welfare contributions during her many years in Japan. While she had often been the target of ridicule and criticism from the Western community in Nagasaki during her early years in Japan, the farewell she received from the foreign residents of Nagasaki upon her retirement also revealed the high stature she and her school had attained since she had established Kwassui forty years earlier. The May 28, 1919, issue of *The Nagasaki Express* newspaper honored Russell's work as the founder of Kwassui, stating that

> [f]or some years progress was slow, but success was achieved and to day [*sic*] Kwassui Jo Gakko has four hundred students and Academy, High School, College, Industrial, Kindergarten, Normal, Bible Women Training, and Music Departments, with a strong staff of American and Japanese teachers. . . . The buildings, which include dormitories for boarders, are splendidly situated and appear to be well-equipped. Kwassui Jo Gakko is a magnificent demonstration of the work of Christian women and particularly of the founder's faith and zeal. (2)

Kwassui continues to thrive as an active educational institution, with programs from junior high school through college. Russell's original school buildings were replaced in 1926. Although badly damaged, the 1926 buildings survived the 1945 atomic bombing of Nagasaki and remain part of the school complex today.

References

Index

References

Abbott, Conda Delite Hitch. 1997. *Envoy of Grace: The Life of Helen Barrett Montgomery.* Valley Forge, Pa.: American Baptist Historical Society.

Akie, Shoko. 1963. "Kirisutokyōkei Joshi Kyōiku Kenkyū no Shiori: Meiji Jidai Purotesutantokei Jogakkō ni tsuite" [Overview of Christian Female Education: Protestant Missionary Schools in the Meiji Era]. *Bungei to Shisō* [Literature and Thought] 25: 51–65.

Alexander, E. Margaret. 1957. *Washington Seminary and Its Influence on the Upper Ohio Valley.* Duplicated. Historical Society of Western Pennsylvania, Pittsburgh.

Araya, Takeshiro, ed. 1976. *Some Works of Mrs. F. B. Harris from "The Heathen Woman's Friend."* Accessed through the United Methodist Archives, Drew University, Madison, N.J.

Auslin, Michael R. 2004. *Negotiating with Imperialism: The Unequal Treaties and the Culture of Japanese Diplomacy.* Cambridge: Harvard Univ. Press.

Bacon, Alice. [1891] 1902. *Japanese Girls and Women.* New York: Houghton Mifflin.

Baker, Frances J. [1896] 1987. *The Story of the Woman's Foreign Missionary Society of the Methodist Episcopal Church, 1869–1895.* Reprint, New York: Garland Publishing.

Baldwin, Esther E. [1881, 1890] 1993. *Must the Chinese Go?: An Examination of the Chinese Question, by Mrs. S.L. Baldwin, Eighteen Years a Missionary in China.* Reprinted in *Racism, Dissent, and Asian Americans from 1850 to the Present: A Documentary History,* edited by Philip S. Foner and Daniel Rosenberg. Westport, Conn.: Greenwood Press.

Ballhatchet, Helen J. 2003. "The Modern Missionary Movement in Japan: Roman Catholic, Protestant, Orthodox." In *Handbook of Christianity in Japan,* edited by Mark R. Mullins, 35–68. Leiden: Brill.

Banks, Louis Albert. 1904. *The Religious Life of Famous Americans.* Boston: American Tract Society.

Barclay, Wade Crawford. 1957. *The Methodist Episcopal Church, 1845–1939*. Vol. 1, *Widening Horizons, 1845–95*. New York: The Board of Missions of the Methodist Church.

Barr, Pat. 1968. *The Deer Cry Pavilion: The Story of Westerners in Japan, 1868–1905*. New York: Harcourt, Brace & World.

Bashford, James W. N.d. "The Bible for Woman Suffrage." New York: National American Woman Suffrage Association. Accessed through the United Methodist Archives, Drew University, Madison, N.J.

———. N.d. *The Bible and Woman*. Chicago: Woman's Temperance Publication Association. Accessed through the United Methodist Archives, Drew University, Madison, N.J.

Bays, Daniel H., and Grant Wacker, eds. 2003. *The Foreign Missionary Enterprise at Home: Explorations in North American Cultural History*. Tuscaloosa: Univ. of Alabama Press.

Beauchamp, Edward R. 1976. *An American Teacher in Early Meiji Japan*. Honolulu: Univ. of Hawai'i Press.

Beauchamp, Edward R., and Akira Iriye, eds. 1990. *Foreign Employees in Nineteenth-Century Japan*. Boulder, Co.: Westview Press.

Beecher, Catharine E. 1841. *A Treatise on Domestic Economy*. Boston: Marsh, Capen, Lyon, and Webb.

Bernstein, Gail Lee, ed. 1991. *Recreating Japanese Women, 1600–1945*. Berkeley: Univ. of California Press.

Bhabha, Homi K. 1994. *The Location of Culture*. London: Routledge.

Bowie, Fiona, Deborah Kirkwood, and Shirley Ardener, eds. 1993. *Women and Missions, Past and Present: Anthropological and Historical Perceptions*. Providence, R.I.: Berg.

Boydston, Jeanne. 1990. *Home and Work: Housework, Wages and the Ideology of Labor in the Early Republic*. New York and Oxford: Oxford Univ. Press.

Brackney, William H. 1991. "The Legacy of Helen B. Montgomery and Lucy W. Peabody." *International Bulletin of Missionary Research* 15, no. 4:174–79.

Branton, Harriet K. 1977. *"Dear Old Sem": The Story of the Washington Female Seminary, 1836–1948*. Duplicated. Accessed through the Historical Society of Western Pennsylvania, Pittsburgh.

Brekus, Catherine A. 2001. "Female Evangelism in the Early Methodist Movement, 1784–1845." In *Methodism and the Shaping of American Culture*, edited by Nathan O. Hatch and John H. Wigger, 135–73. Nashville, Tenn.: Kingswood Books/Abingdon Press.

Buckley, James Monroe. [1891] 1987. *"Because They are Women" and Other Editorials from "The Christian Advocate" on the Admission of Women to the General Conference.* Reprinted in *The Debate in the Methodist Episcopal Church Over Laity Rights for Women*, edited by Carolyn De Swarte Gifford. New York: Garland Publishing.

Burton, Antoinette M. 1990. "The White Woman's Burden: British Feminists and The Indian Woman, 1865–1915." *Women's Studies International Forum* 13, no. 4:295–308.

———. 1994. *Burdens of History: British Feminists, Indian Women, and Imperial Culture, 1865–1915.* Chapel Hill and London: Univ. of North Carolina Press.

Burton, Margaret E. 1914. *The Education of Women in Japan.* New York: Fleming H. Revell.

Butcher, Patricia Smith. 1989. *Education for Equality: Women's Rights Periodicals and Women's Higher Education, 1849–1920.* New York: Greenwood Press.

Butler, Clementina. 1929. *Mrs. William Butler: Two Empires and the Kingdom.* New York: The Methodist Book Concern.

Cary, Otis. [1909] 1993. *The History of Christianity in Modern Japan.* Vol. 2, *Protestant Missions.* Reprint, Surrey, England: Curzon Press.

Cattan, Louise Armstrong. 1972. *Lamps are for Lighting: The Story of Helen Barrett Montgomery and Lucy Waterbury Peabody.* Grand Rapids, Mich.: Eerdmans.

Chaudhuri, Nupur, and Margaret Strobel, eds. 1992. *Western Women and Imperialism: Complicity and Resistance.* Bloomington and Indianapolis: Indiana Univ. Press.

Colquhoun, Archibald R. 1902. *The Mastery of the Pacific.* New York: MacMillan.

Cooper, Frederick, and Ann Laura Stoler, eds. 1997. *Tensions of Empire: Colonial Cultures in a Bourgeois World.* Berkeley: Univ. of California Press.

Cott, Nancy F. 1977. *The Bonds of Womanhood: "Women's Sphere" in New England, 1780–1835.* New Haven, Conn.: Yale Univ. Press.

———, ed. 1993. *History of Women in the United States: Historical Articles on Women's Lives and Activities.* Vol. 12, *Education.* Munich: K. G. Saur.

Couch, Helen. n.d. "Elizabeth Russell, Pioneer of Higher Education for Japanese Women." Cincinnati, Ohio: Woman's Division of Christian Service, Board of Missions and Church Extension, The Methodist Church, Literature Headquarters. Accessed through the Russell Collection, Kwassui Jo Gakuin, Nagasaki, Japan.

Donaldson, Laura E., and Kwok Pui-lan, eds. 2002. *Postcolonialism, Feminism, and Religious Discourse.* New York: Routledge.

DuBois, Ellen Carol. 2000. "Woman Suffrage around the World: Three Phases of Suffragist Internationalism." In *Unequal Sisters: A Multicultural Reader in U.S.*

Women's History, edited by Vicki L. Ruiz and Ellen Carol DuBois, 276–91. 3rd ed. New York: Routledge.

Dustin, Mary E. 1873. "Who Is Our Sister?" *The Heathen Woman's Friend* 5, no. 6: cover page.

Duvall, Sylvanus Milne. 1928. *The Methodist Episcopal Church and Education up to 1869.* New York: Teachers College, Columbia University.

Dyer, Henry. 1904. *Dai Nippon: The Britain of the East.* London: Blackie and Son.

Eder, Elizabeth K. 2003. *Constructing Opportunity: American Women Educators in Early Meiji Japan.* Lanham, Md.: Lexington Books.

Engelman, Karen S. 1990. "A Japanese Missionary School for Girls: Women's Spirituality in the Process of Modernization." Ed.D. Thesis, Columbia University.

Eschbach, Elizabeth Seymour. 1993. *The Higher Education of Women in England and America, 1865–1920.* New York: Garland Publishing.

Fairbank, John King. 1974. *The Missionary Enterprise in China and America.* Cambridge: Harvard Univ. Press.

Fairbanks, A. W., ed. 1898. *Emma Willard and Her Pupils.* New York: Mrs. Russell Sage.

Flemming, Leslie A., ed. 1989. *Women's Work for Women: Missionaries and Social Change in Asia.* Boulder: Westview Press.

Flowers, Montaville. 1917. *The Japanese Conquest of American Opinion.* New York: George H. Doran.

Foner, Philip S., and Daniel Rosenberg, eds. 1993. *Racism, Dissent, and Asian Americans from 1850 to the Present: A Documentary History.* Westport, Conn.: Greenwood Press.

Fones-Wolf, Ken, and Ronald L. Lewis, eds. 2002. *Transnational West Virginia: Ethnic Communities and Economic Change, 1840–1940.* Morgantown: West Virginia Univ. Press.

Frankenberg, Ruth. 1992. *The Social Construction of Whiteness: White Women, Race Matters.* London: Routledge.

Freedman, Estelle. 1979. "Separatism as Strategy: Female Institution Building and American Feminism, 1870–1930." *Feminist Studies* 5, no. 3:512–29.

Fridell, Wilbur M. 1970. "Government Ethics Textbooks in Late Meiji Japan." *The Journal of Asian Studies* 29, no. 4:823–33.

Fujieda, Mioko. 1995. "Japan's First Phase of Feminism." In *Japanese Women: New Feminist Perspectives on the Past, Present and Future,* edited by Kumiko Fujimura-Fanselow and Atsuko Kameda, 323–41. New York: The Feminist Press at CUNY.

Fujimura-Fanselow, Kumiko, and Atsuko Kameda, eds. 1995. *Japanese Women: New Feminist Perspectives on the Past, Present and Future.* New York: The Feminist Press at CUNY.

Fukuda, Hideko. [1904] 1983. *Warawa no hanseigai* [Half My Life]. Reprint, Tokyo: Iwanami Shoten.

Gagan, Rosemary R. 1992. *A Sensitive Independence: Canadian Methodist Women Missionaries in Canada and the Orient, 1881–1925.* Montreal and Kingston: McGill-Queen's Univ. Press.

Gifford, Carolyn De Swarte, ed. 1987. *The Debate in the Methodist Episcopal Church Over Laity Rights for Women.* New York: Garland Publishing.

Ginzberg, Lori D. 2000. *Women in Antebellum Reform.* Wheeling, Ill.: Harlan Davidson.

Gluck, Carol. 1985. *Japan's Modern Myths: Ideology in the Late Meiji Period.* Princeton, N.J.: Princeton Univ. Press.

Gossett, Thomas F. 1997. *Race: A History of an Idea in America.* New ed. New York: Oxford Univ. Press.

Gulick, Sidney L. 1915. *Working Women of Japan.* New York: Missionary Education Movement of the United States and Canada.

Hane, Mikiso. 2003. *Peasants, Rebels, Women, and Outcastes: The Underside of Modern Japan.* 2nd ed. Lanham, Md.: Rowman and Littlefield.

Hara, Kimi. 1995. "Challenges to Education for Girls and Women in Modern Japan: Past and Present." In *Japanese Women: New Feminist Perspectives on the Past, Present and Future,* edited by Kumiko Fujimura-Fanselow and Atsuko Kameda, 93–106. New York: The Feminist Press at CUNY.

Hardesty, Nancy A. 1999. *Women Called to Witness: Evangelical Feminism in the Nineteenth Century.* 2nd ed. Knoxville: Univ. of Tennessee Press.

———. 2003. "The Scientific Study of Missions: Textbooks of the Central Committee on the United Study of Foreign Missions." In *The Foreign Missionary Enterprise at Home: Explorations in North American Cultural History,* edited by Daniel H. Bays and Grant Wacker, 106–22. Tuscaloosa: Univ. of Alabama Press.

Harvey, Fannie Cutler. 1911. "Great Events of a Hundred Years Ago." *Woman's Missionary Friend* 43, no. 2:39–42.

Hastings, Thomas John. 2003. "Japan's Protestant Schools and Churches in Light of Early Mission Theory and History." In *Handbook of Christianity in Japan,* edited by Mark R. Mullins, 101–23. Leiden: Brill.

Hatch, Nathan O. 2001. "The Puzzle of American Methodism." In *Methodism and the Shaping of American Culture,* edited by Nathan O. Hatch and John H. Wigger, 23–40. Nashville: Kingswood Books/Abingdon Press.

Hatch, Nathan O., and John H. Wigger, eds. 2001. *Methodism and the Shaping of American Culture.* Nashville: Kingswood Books/Abington Press.

Hempton, David. 2005. *Methodism: Empire of the Spirit.* New Haven, Conn.: Yale Univ. Press.

Henning, Joseph M. 2000. *Outposts of Civilization: Race, Religion, and the Formative Years of American-Japanese Relations.* New York: New York Univ. Press.

Higham, John. 1969. *From Boundlessness to Consolidation: The Transformation of American Culture, 1848–1860.* Ann Arbor, Mich.: William L. Clements.

Hill, Patricia R. 1985. *The World Their Household: The American Woman's Foreign Mission Movement and Cultural Transformation, 1870–1920.* Ann Arbor: Univ. of Michigan Press.

Hirobe, Izumi. 2001. *Japanese Pride, American Prejudice: Modifying the Exclusion Clause of the 1924 Immigration Act.* Stanford, Calif.: Stanford Univ. Press.

Hobsbawm, E. J. 1987. *The Age of Empire, 1875–1914.* London: Weidenfeld and Nicolson.

Hodgson, C. Pemberton. 1861. *A Residence at Nagasaki and Hakodate in 1859–1860.* London: Richard Bentley, New Burlington Street.

Hoffman, Nancy. 2003. *Woman's "True" Profession: Voices from the History of Teaching.* 2nd ed. Cambridge, Mass.: Harvard Education Press.

Honda, Yoichi. 1909. "Japanese Religious Beliefs: Christianity." In *Fifty Years of New Japan,* vol. 2, edited by Shigenobu Ōkuma. London: Smith, Elder, and Co.

Hoskins, Mrs. Robert. 1912. *Clara A. Swain, M.D., First Medical Missionary to the Women of the Orient.* Boston: WFMS.

Huber, Mary Taylor, and Nancy C. Lutkehaus, eds. 1999. *Gendered Missions: Women and Men in Missionary Discourse and Practice.* Ann Arbor: Univ. of Michigan Press.

Hughey, George W. [1891] 1987. *The Admission of Women to the General Conference: A Reply to Dr. Buckley's Pamphlet "Because They are Women," and Other Editorials.* Reprinted in *The Debate in the Methodist Episcopal Church Over Laity Rights for Women,* edited by Carolyn De Swarte Gifford. New York: Garland Publishing.

Hunter, Jane. 1984. *The Gospel of Gentility: American Women Missionaries in Turn-of-the-Century China.* New Haven: Yale Univ. Press.

Hutchison, William R. 1987. *Errand to the World: American Protestant Thought and Foreign Missions.* Chicago: Univ. of Chicago Press.

HWF. See *The Heathen Woman's Friend* under Woman's Foreign Missionary Society of the Methodist Episcopal Church.

Ing, Lucy. 1875. "Notes from Japan." *The Heathen Woman's Friend* 6, no. 10:839–42.

Iriye, Akira. 1975. "Japan as a Competitor, 1895–1917." In *Mutual Images: Essays in American-Japanese Relations,* edited by Akira Iriye, 73–99. Cambridge, Mass.: Harvard Univ. Press.

Irokawa, Daikichi. 1985. *The Culture of the Meiji Period.* Princeton, N.J.: Princeton Univ. Press.

Isham, Mary. 1936. *Valorous Ventures: A Record of Sixty and Six Years of the Woman's Foreign Missionary Society, Methodist Episcopal Church.* Boston: WFMS.

Ishii, Noriko Kawamura. 2004. *American Women Missionaries at Kobe College, 1873–1909.* New York and London: Routledge.

Jansen, Marius B. 1995. *The Emergence of Meiji Japan.* Cambridge: Cambridge Univ. Press.

Japan Evangelist, The. 1893–1900. Yokohama: Yokohama Seishi Bunsha. Accessed through the Aoyama Gakuin Archives, Tokyo, Japan.

Johnson, Mrs. F. I. 1929. "Elizabeth Russell Who Went to Japan." In *The One Who Went and the One She Found: A Book of Adventures.* Boston: WFMS. Accessed through the Russell Collection, Kwassui Gakuin, Nagasaki, Japan.

Kaneko, Sachiko. 1995. "The Struggle for Legal Rights and Reforms: A Historical View." In *Japanese Women: New Feminist Perspectives on the Past, Present and Future,* edited by Kumiko Fujimura-Fanselow and Atsuko Kameda, 3–14. New York: The Feminist Press at CUNY.

Katoh, Masao. 1996. *Meijiki Kirisutosha no Seishin to Gendai: Kirisutokyōkei Gakkō ga Sōritsu* [The Spirit of the Meiji Christians and Modernity: Christian Schools Are Founded]. Tokyo: Kindai Bungeisha.

Keller, Rosemary Skinner. 1993. *Spirituality and Social Responsibility: Vocational Vision of Women in the United Methodist Tradition.* Nashville: Abingdon Press.

Kelsky, Karen. 1996. "The Gender Politics of Women's Internationalism in Japan." *International Journal of Politics, Culture and Society* 10, no. 1:29–51.

———. 2001. *Women on the Verge: Japanese Women, Western Dreams.* Durham, N.C.: Duke Univ. Press.

Kerber, Linda K. 1997. *Toward an Intellectual History of Women: Essays.* Chapel Hill: Univ. of North Carolina.

Kinmonth, Earl H. 1981. *The Self-Made Man in Meiji Japanese Thought: From Samurai to Salary Man.* Berkeley: Univ. of California Press.

Kiyooka, Eiichi, ed. 1988. *Fukuzawa Yukichi on Japanese Women: Selected Works.* Tokyo: Univ. of Tokyo Press.

Knowles, James D. [1831] 1987. *Memoir of Mrs. Ann H. Judson, Late Missionary to Burmah.* 4th ed. Reprint, New York: Garland Publishing.

Kodansha Encyclopedia of Japan. 1983. New York: Kodansha.

Kohiyama, Rui. 1992. *Amerika Fujin Senkyōshi: Rainichi no Haikei to Sono Eikyō* [As Our God Alone Will Lead Us: The Nineteenth-Century American Women's Mission Enterprise and Its Encounter with Meiji Japan]. Tokyo: Tokyo Daigaku Shuppankai.

Krummel, John W. 1973. "Methodist Beginnings in Japan: Part One." *Methodist History* 11, no. 2:3–19.

———. 1973. "Methodist Beginnings in Japan: Part Two." *Methodist History* 11, no. 3:3–51.

———. 1995. "A Directory of Bible Women of the Japan Methodist Protestant Church 1880–1940." *Aoyama Journal of General Education* 36:15–28.

Kume, Kunitake. [1878] 1985. *Tokumei Zenken Taishi Bei-Ō Kairan Jikki* (A True Account of the Ambassador Extraordinary and Plenipotentiary's Journey of Observation Through the United States of America and Europe). 5 vols. Edited by Akira Tanaka. Reprint, Tokyo: Iwanami Shoten.

Kwassui Gakuin Hyakunenshi Hensan Iinkai, ed. 1980. *Kwassui Gakuin Hyakunenshi* [The Centennial History of Kwassui Gakuin]. Nagasaki: Kwassui Gakuin. Accessed through the Russell Collection, Kwassui Gakuin, Nagasaki, Japan.

Kwassui Jo Gakko: 1879–1929. 1929. Fiftieth Anniversary Bulletin. N.p. Accessed through the Russell Collection, Kwassui Gakuin, Nagasaki, Japan.

Kwassui Nanajugonen no Ayumi [Seventy-five-year History of Kwassui]. 1954. Nagasaki: Kwassui Gakuin. Accessed through the Russell Collection, Kwassui Gakuin, Nagasaki, Japan.

Kwok, Pui-lan. 1992. *Chinese Women and Christianity, 1860–1927.* Atlanta: Scholars Press.

———. 2002. "Unbinding Our Feet: Saving Brown Women and Feminist Religious Discourse." In *Postcolonialism, Feminism, and Religious Discourse,* edited by Laura E. Donaldson and Kwok Pui-lan, 62–81. New York: Routledge.

Lian, Xi. 1997. *The Conversion of Missionaries: Liberalism in American Protestant Missions in China, 1907–1932.* University Park: Pennsylvania State Univ. Press.

Lindley, Susan Hill. 1996. *"You Have Stept Out of Your Place": A History of Women and Religion in America.* Louisville, Ky.: Westminster John Knox Press.

Long, Kathryn T. 2001. "Consecrated Respectability: Phoebe Palmer and the Refinement of American Methodism." In *Methodism and the Shaping of American Culture,* edited by Nathan O. Hatch and John H. Wigger, 281–307. Nashville, Tenn.: Kingswood Books/Abingdon Press.

Lord, John. 1873. *The Life of Emma Willard.* New York: D. Appleton.

Lutz, Alma. 1929. *Emma Willard: Daughter of Democracy.* Boston: Houghton Mifflin.

Mackie, Vera. 2003. *Feminism in Modern Japan: Citizenship, Embodiment, and Sexuality.* Cambridge: Cambridge Univ. Press.

Marshall, Byron. 1994. *Learning to be Modern: Japanese Political Discourse on Education.* Boulder, Co.: Westview Press.

Matthew Simpson Papers. Accessed through the United Methodist Archives, Drew University, Madison, N.J.

McCreary, Patricia. 1992. "Realms of Glory: The Life of Elizabeth Russell." Duplicated. Accessed through the Russell Collection, Kwassui Gakuin, Nagasaki, Japan.

McDonald, W., and John E. Searles. [1885] 1985. *The Life of Rev. John S. Inskip.* Reprint, New York: Garland Publishing.

MEC. See Methodist Episcopal Church.

Methodist Episcopal Church (MEC). 1886–1924. *Minutes of the Woman's Conference of the Methodist Episcopal Church in Japan.* Yokohama: Japan Publishing Agency; Fukuin Printing Company; various publishers. Accessed through the Aoyama Gakuin Archives, Tokyo, Japan.

———. 1903. *Minutes of the Woman's Annual Conference of the Methodist Episcopal Church in South Japan.* N.p. Accessed through the Russell Collection, Kwassui Gakuin, Nagasaki, Japan.

———, Japan Mission. 1898–1905. *Tidings from Japan (TFJ).* Tokyo: David S. Spencer. Accessed through the Aoyama Gakuin Archives, Tokyo, Japan.

Missionary Society of the Methodist Episcopal Church (MSMEC). 1873–99. Annual Reports. New York: MSMEC. Accessed through Aoyama Gakuin Archives, Tokyo, Japan.

Miura, Hiroshi. 1996. *The Life and Thought of Kanzō Uchimura, 1861–1930.* Grand Rapids, Mich.: W. B. Eerdmans.

Miyazaki, Kentarō. 2003. "The Kakure Kirishitan Tradition." In *Handbook of Christianity in Japan,* edited by Mark R. Mullins, 19–34. Leiden: Brill.

Mobley, Kendal P. 2003. "The Ecumenical Woman's Missionary Movement: Helen Barrett Montgomery and the Baptist, 1920–30." In *Gender and the Social Gospel,* edited by Wendy J. Deichmann Edwards and Carolyn De Swarte Gifford, 167–81. Urbana: Univ. of Illinois Press.

Molony, Barbara. 2000. "Women's Rights, Feminism, and Suffragism in Japan, 1870–1925." *Pacific Historical Review* 69, no. 4:639–63.

Montgomery, Helen Barrett. 1894. "Equal Suffrage." *Harper's Bazar* 27, no. 18 (May 5): 354–55.

———. 1909. *The Empire of the East.* Chicago: A. C. McClurg.

———. 1910. *Western Women in Eastern Lands.* New York: MacMillan.

———. 1940. *Helen Barrett Montgomery: From Campus to World Citizenship.* New York: Revell.

Moorhead, James H. 1999. *World without End: Mainstream American Protestant Visions of the Last Things, 1880–1925.* Bloomington: Indiana Univ. Press.

Mori, Arinori. 1873. *Education in Japan: A Series of Letters Addressed by Prominent Americans to Arinori Mori.* New York: D. Appleton.

Mountford, Roxanne. 2003. *The Gendered Pulpit: Preaching in American Protestant Spaces.* Carbondale: Southern Illinois Univ. Press.

MSMEC. See Missionary Society of the Methodist Episcopal Church.

Mullins, Mark. 1998. *Christianity Made in Japan: A Study of Indigenous Movements.* Honolulu: Univ. of Hawai'i Press.

———, ed. 2003. *Handbook of Christianity in Japan.* Leiden: Brill.

Muta, Kazue. 1994. "Images of the Family in Meiji Periodicals: The Paradox Underlying the Emergence of the 'Home.'" *U.S.-Japan Women's Journal English Supplement* 7:53–71.

Najita, Tetsuo. 1974. *The Intellectual Foundations of Modern Japanese Politics.* Chicago: Univ. of Chicago Press.

Nihon Kirisutokyō Fujin Kyōfūkai, ed. 1986. *Nihon Kirisutokyō Fujin Kyōfūkai Hyakunenshi* [A History of the First Hundred Years of the Japan Christian Women's Temperance Union]. Tokyo: Domesu Shuppan.

Nitobe, Inazō. 1909. "The Influence of the West upon Japan." In *Fifty Years of New Japan,* vol. 2, edited by Shigenobu Ōkuma. London: Smith, Elder, and Co.

Nolte, Sharon, and Sally Hastings. 1991. "The Meiji State's Policy toward Women, 1890–1910." In *Recreating Japanese Women, 1600–1945,* edited by Gail Lee Bernstein, 151–74. Berkeley: Univ. of California Press.

Notehelfer, F. G. 1985. *American Samurai: Captain L. L. Janes and Japan.* Princeton, N.J.: Princeton Univ. Press.

Nott, Josiah C. [1849] 1969. "Two Lectures on the Connection between the Biblical and Physical History of Man." Reprint, New York: Negro Universities Press.

Ogawa, Manako. 2004. "'Hull-House' in Downtown Tokyo: The Transplantation of a Settlement House from the United States into Japan and the North American Missionary Women, 1919–1945." *Journal of World History* 15, no. 3:359–87.

Ōkuma, Shigenobu, ed. 1909. *Fifty Years of New Japan.* Vol. 2. London: Smith, Elder, and Co.

Oldham, William F. 1902. *Isabella Thoburn.* Chicago: Jennings & Pye.

One Who Went and the One She Found, The: A Book of Adventures. 1929. Boston: WFMS. Accessed through the Russell Collection, Kwassui Gakuin, Nagasaki, Japan.

Papanek, Hanna. 1977. "Development Planning for Women." In *Women and National Development: The Complexities of Change,* edited by the Wellesley Editorial Committee, Center for Research on Women in Higher Education and the Professions, Wellesley College, 14–21. Chicago: Univ. of Chicago Press.

Pierson, John D. 1980. *Tokutomi Sohō, 1863–1957: A Journalist for Modern Japan.* Princeton, N.J.: Princeton Univ. Press.

Porterfield, Amanda. 1997. *Mary Lyon and the Mount Holyoke Missionaries.* New York: Oxford Univ. Press.

Proceedings of the General Conference of Protestant Missionaries in Japan held in Tokyo, October 24–31, 1900, with Extensive Supplements. 1901. Tokyo: Methodist Pub. House.

Pyle, Kenneth B. 1969. *The New Generation in Meiji Japan: Problems of Cultural Identity, 1885–1895.* Stanford, Calif.: Stanford Univ. Press.

Quarter-Centennial Re-Union of the Graduates of the Washington Female Seminary, 1866. 1866. N.p. Accessed through the Historical Society of Western Pennsylvania, Pittsburgh, Pa.

Reid, J. M., and J. T. Gracey. 1895. *Missions and Missionary Society of the Methodist Episcopal Church.* Rev. ed. New York: Hunt and Eaton.

Reischauer, Edwin O. 1990. *Japan: The Story of a Nation.* 4th ed. New York: McGraw-Hill.

Richey, Russell E. 1996. *The Methodist Conference in America: A History.* Nashville, Tenn.: Kingswood Books/Abingdon Press.

———. 2003. "Organizing for Missions: A Methodist Case Study." In *The Foreign Missionary Enterprise at Home: Explorations in North American Cultural History,* edited by Daniel H. Bays and Grant Wacker, 75–89. Tuscaloosa: Univ. of Alabama Press.

Richey, Russell E., Kenneth E. Rowe, and Jean Miller Schmidt, eds. 1993. *Perspectives on American Methodism: Interpretive Essays.* Nashville, Tenn.: Kingswood Books/Abingdon Press.

Robert, Dana L. 1996. *American Women in Mission: A Social History of Their Thought and Practice.* Macon, Ga.: Mercer Univ. Press.

———. 2002. "The Influence of American Missionary Women on the World Back Home." *Religion and American Culture: A Journal of Interpretation* 12, no. 1:59–90.

Robins-Mowry, Dorothy. 1989. "Not a Foreigner, But a Sensei." In *Women's Work for Women: Missionaries and Social Change,* edited by Leslie A. Fleming. Boulder, Co.: Westview Press.

———. 1990. "Westernizing Influences in the Early Modernization of Japanese Women's Education." In *Foreign Employees in Nineteenth-Century Japan,* edited by Edward R. Beauchamp and Akira Iriye. Boulder, Co.: Westview Press.

Rose, Barbara. 1992. *Tsuda Umeko and Women's Education in Japan.* New Haven: Yale Univ. Press.

Ruiz, Vicki L., and Ellen Carol DuBois, eds. 2000. *Unequal Sisters: A Multicultural Reader in U.S. Women's History.* 3rd ed. New York: Routledge.

Russell, Elizabeth. 1876. "The Faultless Offering." *The Heathen Woman's Friend* 7, no. 10:227–29.

———. Letters to Emma Tolbert. Accessed through the Russell Collection, Kwassui Gakuin, Nagasaki, Japan.

———. Personal journal. Accessed through the Russell Collection, Kwassui Gakuin, Nagasaki, Japan.

———. N.d. "Pioneer Days in My Beloved Japan." Boston: WFMS. Accessed through the Russell Collection, Kwassui Gakuin, Nagasaki, Japan.

Ryan, Mary P. 1990. *Women in Public: Between Banners and Ballots, 1825–1880.* Baltimore: Johns Hopkins Univ. Press.

Said, Edward W. 1979. *Orientalism.* New York: Vintage Books.

———. 1993. *Culture and Imperialism.* New York: Vintage Books.

Sand, Jordan. 1998. "At Home in the Meiji Period: Inventing Japanese Domesticity." In *Mirror of Modernity: Invented Traditions of Modern Japan,* edited by Stephen Vlastos, 191–207. Berkeley: Univ. of California Press.

Scheiner, Irwin. 1970. *Christian Converts and Social Protest in Meiji Japan.* Berkeley: Univ. of California Press.

Schmidt, Jean Miller. 1993. "Reexamining the Public/Private Split: Reforming the Continent and Spreading Scriptural Holiness." In *Perspectives on American Methodism: Interpretive Essays,* edited by Russell E. Richey, Kenneth E. Rowe, and Jean Miller Schmidt, 228–47. Nashville, Tenn.: Kingswood Books/Abingdon Press.

———. 1999. *Grace Sufficient: A History of Women in American Methodism, 1760–1939.* Nashville, Tenn.: Abingdon Press.

Schneider, Gregory. 1993. *The Way of the Cross Leads Home: The Domestication of American Methodism.* Bloomington: Indiana Univ. Press.

Schueller, Malini Johar. 1998. *U.S. Orientalisms: Race, Nation, and Gender in Literature, 1790–1890.* Ann Arbor: Univ. of Michigan Press.

Scott, Anne Firor. 1978. "What, Then, Is the American: This New Woman?" *Journal of American History* 65:679–703.

———. 1979. "The Ever-Widening Circle: The Diffusion of Feminist Values from the Troy Female Seminary, 1822–72." *History of Education Quarterly* 19:3–25.

Scott, Joan. 1988. *Gender and the Politics of History.* New York: Columbia Univ. Press.

Seat, Karen K. 2003. "Mission Schools and Education for Women." In *Handbook of Christianity in Japan,* edited by Mark R. Mullins, 321–42. Leiden: Brill.

Shakespeare, William. [1603] 1987. *Hamlet.* In *The Complete Works of Shakespeare, From the Original Text.* Reprint, Secaucus, N.J.: Wellfleet Press.

Shively, Donald. 1971. "The Japanization of the Middle Meiji." In *Tradition and Modernization in Japanese Culture,* edited by Donald Shively, 77–119. Princeton, N.J.: Princeton Univ. Press.

Sievers, Sharon L. 1983. *Flowers in Salt: The Beginnings of Feminist Consciousness in Modern Japan.* Stanford, Calif.: Stanford Univ. Press.

Simpson, Matthew. 1873. "Woman's Suffrage" (speech delivered on February 7). Matthew Simpson Papers, the United Methodist Archives, Drew University, Madison, N.J.

Singh, Maina Chawla. 2000. *Gender, Religion, and "Heathen Lands": American Missionary Women in South Asia (1860s–1940s).* New York: Garland Publishing.

Sklar, Kathryn Kish. 1973. *Catharine Beecher: A Study in American Domesticity.* New Haven: Yale Univ. Press.

Smith-Rosenberg, Carroll. 1986. *Disorderly Conduct: Visions of Gender in Victorian America.* New York: Oxford Univ. Press.

Solomon, Barbara Miller. 1985. *In the Company of Educated Women: A History of Women and Higher Education in America.* New Haven: Yale Univ. Press.

Soviak, Eugene. 1971. "On the Nature of Western Progress: The Journal of the Iwakura Embassy." In *Tradition and Modernization in Japanese Culture,* edited by Donald Shively. Princeton, N.J.: Princeton Univ. Press.

Stanley, Amy Dru. 1996. "Home Life and the Morality of the Market." In *The Market Revolution in America: Social, Political, and Religious Expressions, 1800–1880,* edited by Melvyn Stokes and Stephen Conway. Charlottesville: Univ. of Virginia Press.

Stearns, Peter N. 1991. *Interpreting the Industrial Revolution.* Washington, D.C.: American Historical Association.

———. 1998. *The Industrial Revolution in World History.* Boulder, Co.: Westview Press.

Steiner, Jesse Frederick. 1917. *The Japanese Invasion: A Study in the Psychology of Inter-Racial Contacts.* Chicago: A. C. McClurg.

Sterry, Lorraine. 2003. "Constructs of Meiji Japan: The Role of Writing by Victorian Women Travellers." *Japanese Studies* 23, no. 2:167–83.

Stokes, Melvin, and Stephen Conway, eds. 1996. *The Market Revolution in America: Social, Political, and Religious Expressions, 1800–1880*. Charlottesville: Univ. of Virginia Press.

Stone, Lucy. Letters to Bishop Matthew Simpson dated May 3, 1869, and July 27, 1874. Matthew Simpson Papers, the United Methodist Archives, Drew University, Madison, N.J.

Takaki, Ronald. 1998. *Strangers from a Different Shore: A History of Asian Americans*. Rev. ed. Boston: Little, Brown.

Taylor, Sandra C. 1979. "The Sisterhood of Salvation and the Sunrise Kingdom: Congregational Women Missionaries in Meiji Japan." *Pacific Historical Review* 48 (February): 27–45.

Telford, John. 1895. *Women in the Mission Field: Glimpses of Christian Women among the Heathen*. London: C. H. Kelly.

Thelen, David. 1999. "The Nation and Beyond: Transnational Perspectives on United States History." *The Journal of American History* 86, no. 3:965–75.

Thoburn, J. M. 1903. *Life of Isabella Thoburn*. Cincinnati: Jennings and Pye; New York: Eaton and Mains.

Tocco, Martha Caroline. 1995. "School Bound: Women's Higher Education in Nineteenth Century Japan." Ph.D. Thesis. Stanford Univ.

Tonkovich, Nicole. 1997. *Domesticity with a Difference: The Nonfiction of Catharine Beecher, Sarah J. Hale, Fanny Fern, and Margaret Fuller*. Jackson: Univ. Press of Mississippi.

Tsunoda, Ryusaku, Wm. Theodore de Bary, and Donald Keene, eds. 1958. *Sources of Japanese Tradition*. Vol. 2. New York: Columbia Univ. Press.

Tucker, Ruth A. 1988. *Guardians of the Great Commission: The Story of Women in Modern Missions*. Grand Rapids, Mich.: Academie Books.

Tyrrell, Ian R. 1991. *Woman's World, Woman's Empire: The Woman's Christian Temperance Union in International Perspective, 1800–1930*. Chapel Hill: Univ. of North Carolina Press.

Uno, Kathleen S. 1991. "Women and Changes in the Household Division of Labor." In *Recreating Japanese Women, 1600–1945*, edited by Gail Lee Bernstein, 17–41. Berkeley: Univ. of California Press.

———. 1995. "The Origins of 'Good Wife, Wise Mother.'" In *Japanische Frauengeschichte(n)*, edited by Erich Pauer and Regine Mathias, 31–46. Marburg, Germany: Forderverein Marburger Japan-Reihe.

———. 1999. *Passages to Modernity: Motherhood, Childhood, and Social Reform in Early Twentieth Century Japan*. Honolulu: Univ. of Hawai'i Press.

Vlastos, Stephen, ed. 1998. *Mirror of Modernity: Invented Traditions of Modern Japan.* Berkeley: Univ. of California Press.

Walls, Andrew F. 1996. *The Missionary Movement in Christian History: Studies in the Transmission of Faith.* Maryknoll, N.Y.: Orbis Books.

WBM. See Women's Board of Missions, Congregational Church.

Welter, Barbara. 1966. "The Cult of True Womanhood, 1820–1860." *American Quarterly* 18, no. 2, part 1:151–74.

———. 1978. "She Hath Done What She Could: Protestant Women's Missionary Careers in Nineteenth-Century America." *American Quarterly* 30, no. 5:624–38.

WFMS. See Woman's Foreign Missionary Society of the Methodist Episcopal Church.

WFMSPC. See Woman's Foreign Missionary Society of the Presbyterian Church.

Wheeler, Mary Sparkes. 1884. *First Decade of the Woman's Foreign Missionary Society of the Methodist Episcopal Church, With Sketches of its Missionaries.* New York: Phillips and Hunt; Cincinnati: Cranston and Stowe.

White, Charles Edward. 1986. *The Beauty of Holiness: Phoebe Palmer as Theologian, Revivalist, Feminist, and Humanitarian.* Grand Rapids, Mich.: F. Asbury Press.

Whitney, Clara A. N. 1979. *Clara's Diary: An American Girl in Meiji Japan.* Edited by M. William Steele and Tamiko Ichimata. Tokyo: Kodansha International.

Wigger, John H. 1998. *Taking Heaven by Storm: Methodism and the Rise of Popular Christianity in America.* New York: Oxford Univ. Press.

Willard, Emma. [1819] 1987. *An Address to the Public, Particularly to the Members of the Legislature of New-York, Proposing a Plan for Improving Female Education.* Reprint, Marietta, Ga.: Larlin Corporation.

Willard, Frances. [1888] 1987. *Woman in the Pulpit.* Reprinted in *The Defense of Women's Rights to Ordination in the Methodist Episcopal Church,* edited by Carolyn De Swarte Gifford. New York: Garland Publishing.

WMF. See *Woman's Missionary Friend* under Woman's Foreign Missionary Society of the Methodist Episcopal Church.

Women's Board of Missions, Congregational Church (WBM). 1872. Fourth Annual Report. Boston: WBM.

———. 1869–72. *Life and Light for Heathen Women.* Boston: WBM. Accessed through the Library of Congress, Washington, D.C.

———. 1872–1922. *Life and Light for Woman.* Boston: WBM. Accessed through the Library of Congress, Washington, D.C.

Woman's Foreign Missionary Society of the Methodist Episcopal Church (WFMS). 1882–91. Annual Reports. Boston: WFMS. Accessed through the Aoyama Gakuin Archives, Tokyo, Japan.

———. 1869–95. *The Heathen Woman's Friend (HWF)*. Boston: WFMS. Accessed through the United Methodist Archives, Drew Univ., Madison, N.J.

———. 1896–1924. *Woman's Missionary Friend (WMF)*. Boston: WFMS. Accessed through the United Methodist Archives, Drew Univ., Madison, N.J.

Woman's Foreign Missionary Society of the Presbyterian Church (WFMSPC). 1886. *Woman's Work for Woman and Our Mission Field.* Philadelphia: Woman's Foreign Missionary Society of the Presbyterian Church. Accessed through the Library of Congress, Washington, D.C.

———. 1871–1924. *Woman's Work for Woman (WWW)*. Philadelphia: Woman's Foreign Missionary Society of the Presbyterian Church. Accessed through the Library of Congress, Washington, D.C.

WWW. See *Woman's Work for Woman* under Woman's Foreign Missionary Society of the Presbyterian Church.

Yasutake, Rumi. 2004. *Transnational Women's Activism: The United States, Japan, and Japanese Immigrant Communities in California, 1859–1920.* New York: New York Univ. Press.

Yokoyama, Toshio. 1987. *Japan in the Victorian Mind: A Study of Stereotyped Images of a Nation, 1850–80.* London: Macmillan.

Zink-Sawyer, Beverly Ann. 2003. *From Preachers to Suffragists: Woman's Rights and Religious Conviction in the Lives of Three Nineteenth-Century American Clergywomen.* Louisville: Westminster John Knox Press.

Index